MANPOWER PLANNING
A BIBLIOGRAPHY

MANPOWER PLANNING
A BIBLIOGRAPHY

Edited by C. G. Lewis

In collaboration with
D. J. Bell, D. J. Bryant, A. F. Forbes,
W. R. Hawes, C. S. Leicester,
Rosemary Medlar, A. L. Oliver,
C. J. Purkiss, G. A. Yewdall

THE ENGLISH UNIVERSITIES PRESS LTD
ST. PAUL'S HOUSE WARWICK LANE
LONDON EC4

Ref.
Z
7164
.b1
b42

First printed 1969

SBN 340 05263 5

Printed and Bound in Great Britain for
The English Universities Press Ltd, by
C. Tinling & Co. Ltd, London and Prescot

CONTENTS

PREFACE

This Bibliography is intended to meet the need for a standard reference on Manpower Planning. It can be used by those working at either National, Industry, or Company level.

Manpower Planning is an activity in which one tries to use human resources as effectively and efficiently as possible. This is done by drawing upon the ideas and techniques of many disciplines; among those which have contributed are applied economics, computer science, operational research, personnel management, psychology and statistics. In practice, the solution of any one problem requires a combination of such disciplines.

The book has been set out in two parts:

(i) Commentaries dealing with the various problem areas at the three levels of manpower planning—national, industry, and company level.

(ii) An alphabetic Index of references.

It has been constructed in this way rather than on the basis of individual disciplines because we felt that the reader would find it easier to identify work related to his needs.

Not all the items cited in the Bibliography are mentioned in the Commentaries. The text describes work which has been done at the three levels and indicates gaps which, at present, exist in our knowledge—both in data and techniques—and which need to be filled.

The bibliography has been confined to works in English; several specialised works have been omitted, as have publications which are not easily obtainable through a good library.

This book has been produced by a small team of members of the Manpower Planning Study Group of the Operational Research Society. We wish to express our thanks to the committee of this Study Group for their support and continuing interest. The commentaries have been written by members of this group as indicated in the individual chapters. The task of editing the commentaries and the bibliography was undertaken by C. G. Lewis, of the Statistics Directorate of the Ministry of Defence. The other members of the group and their companies or employers are:

D. J. Bell—Gillette Industries Ltd. (formerly with Central Electricity Generating Board).

D. J. Bryant—Institute for Operational Research.

A. F. Forbes—University of Kent at Canterbury.

W. R. Hawes—

C. S. Leicester—Department of Applied Economics, University of Cambridge.

Rosemary Medlar—Central Statistical Office.

A. L. Oliver—Ministry of Defence.

C. J. Purkiss—International Systems Research Ltd. (formerly with BISRA Ltd.).

G. A. Yewdall—PPBS Associates Ltd. (formerly with Engineering Industry Training Board).

CHAPTER ONE

MANPOWER PLANNING AT THE NATIONAL LEVEL

C. S. Leicester

1 INTRODUCTION

A great deal of manpower planning has gone on in different parts of the world during the last two decades. However we measure the magnitude of this activity or point to examples of it, a lot has taken place. It has been tried in centrally planned economies [512] and in Eastern Europe [435]; and notably in Czechoslovakia [525], Hungary [570] and Russia [527]. It has also been attempted, in one way or another, in some countries of Western Europe: In Austria [534], Britain [601], Eire [409], France [664], Germany [69], Italy [555], the Netherlands [484], Norway [513] and Sweden [491]. Other experience has accumulated as a result of the OECD's Mediterannean Regional Project [417], and in Australia [272], Pakistan [56], India [89], Turkey [579], the United States [654].

The immediate lesson is clear. Any country may benefit from another's manpower planning activity simply by noticing how the latter differs from its own. Some of these differences, admittedly, result from the different objectives, institutions and policies adopted by individual nations. Such features must remain unique to the country concerned. In looking abroad, accordingly, the national manpower planner has to decide which part of other people's practices he may not wish to emulate. This is a negative yield.

But there is also something positive that can be gained by taking an inventory of what was done; and this comes about in two forms. First, we may learn of approaches attempted and techniques tried, whose past success may be duplicated if one cares to use them. Second, we may also realise in which directions we may both expect and desire the methods used to develop in the future.

In taking stock of the position to date, then, this commentary adopts both purposes: to provide information for those concerned with the application of manpower planning techniques, as well as for those concerned with their improvement. In doing so, it abstracts from the diversity of manpower planning practice referred to above, and focusses attention instead on the common features of the techniques which can be imported, willy-nilly, whatever their source of origin. However, this survey makes no claim to omniscience; the literature on manpower planning at the level of the economy is considerably more extensive than the references that follow. This survey is selective, in the sense that ease of accessibility in the English language was a dual criterion adopted. As it is, certain common themes seem to be widely prevalent.

The first is a recognition of the main objective of macro-economic planning. As loosely defined by Lester [336], this is the guidance of changing employment patterns towards desired goals. Such a definition explicitly contains the notion that actual employment patterns—observed in the past and realised in the future—might differ substantially from other desirable employment patterns; and the further notion that action on the part of individuals (in their career choices), on the part of employers (in their use of labour) and on the part of government (over a wide range of matters) could intervene, as stated by Mangum and Nemore [357]. Discerning a future gap between actual and desired patterns demands foresight; and forecasting is an essential part of manpower planning. Discerning a past gap between actual and desired patterns demands analysis; and the measurement of misutilisation is also central to manpower planning. One way of spelling out the implications of the main objective is given by Leicester in [333].

The second recurring theme is that this activity should be linked to two others: economic planning and educational planning. Economic planning, for example, indicates what national goals make certain employment patterns desirable in the future. And the methodology for drawing up economic plans, surveyed in [548], indicates at what stage in the exercise the manpower planner enters upon the scene. The viewpoint, that manpower plans cannot plausibly be drawn up aloof from economic plans, is expressed by Alterman [7], Bhalla [56], Crossley [135], Leicester [334], Paukert [436], Peacock [441] and Sheppard [503], among many others. Educational planning is a different activity, and is concerned with the desired expansion of the education and training system of a country; some people argue it should be geared to providing the manpower needs of the economy, provided the latter are stated in meaningful terms. The need for doing so is expressed quite strongly by Parnes [430–431], while the obstacles met in attempting this link are examined by Hollister [249], Moser and Layard [390] and Bereday, Blaug and Lauwerys [52]. In a general way, therefore, we see that national planning becomes the province of the manpower expert when concern switches from economic variables to labour variables; and ceases to be so whenever manpower crosses the boundary between active employment and economic inactivity (e.g. enters education and training).

The third recurring theme is a methodological one. At some stage, the literature draws attention to five distinct but related parts of this activity. Drawing up a viable manpower plan seems to require: the use of an accounting framework; the projection of manpower needs; the projection of manpower availabilities; the analysis of utilisation; and the monitoring of labour mobility. We shall consider each of these in turn.

2 THE FRAMEWORK OF DEMOGRAPHIC ACCOUNTS

Accounting concepts are useful because of their comprehensive nature; a balance sheet of manpower stocks, disaggregated into mutually exclusive categories, gives a complete picture of the position at one date. Between two dates, the inflows into and the outflows from each category of the balance sheet give an unambiguous measure of the net change in each labour stock. At the target year, the use of an accounting framework ensures that the manpower plan—whatever are its other qualities—at least adds up.

A loose use of accounting identities occurs frequently throughout the literature: see for example [207] and [435]. An explicit definition of a framework for all demographic variables is given by Stone [547], who later made an algebraic statement of a series of interlocking accounts, where inflows into stock at one date unequalled outflows from stock [549]. A symbolic picture, showing the different categories of the full demographic accounts, was detailed by Leicester [333], while a blank tabular representation of parts of the balance sheet was made by the OECD [420], to show what such tables might look like, given the data. Stone [549] has begun to process existing records, in an initial attempt to set up demographic accounts.

It is clear, however, that large gaps exist in the statistics of both flows and stocks of manpower. Many recommendations as to the improvement of these statistics, such as that by Crossley [134] and O'Herlighy [422] pay attention mainly to stocks. The OECD [420] places the necessary heavy emphasis on the need for new flow statistics. We could expect improvements along both fronts in the future. Stone [550] has developed a conceptual framework of demographic accounts that suggests which additional data would be most useful for the purposes of both manpower and educational planning.

3 THE PROJECTION OF MANPOWER NEEDS

No problem has attracted greater attention than that of forecasting the desired future pattern of employment. Symposia that have been organised around this subject include [209, 270, 411, 421, 510]. Individual views and approaches worth noting are [139, 214, 379, 497]. The main topics discussed are the following.
(i) **Techniques of projection.** An excellent survey is given by Johnston [285] who not only takes the reader through the jungle of concepts (e.g. forecast, prediction, projection), but also discusses both qualitative and quantitative techniques. Comparisons between various quantitative techniques only appear frequently elsewhere, and two useful summaries are given by Crossley [135], and the OECD [420]. The evaluation of these techniques on their merits is also often made. For example, Srivastava [530] argues that expediency created by lack of data often dictates a choice; Goldstein and Swerdloff [207] are in favour of a complementary use of many techniques, to double-check calculations; and Leicester [329, 334] suggests there may be unique situations when one or other has the optimum pay-off. For present purposes, these quantitative techniques may be grouped into four categories, and examples of their applications follow.
(a) *Time-series extrapolations*. A single variable may be projected along simple [139] or complicated time trends [620]; or a number of variables may be so projected before being combined (e.g. multiplied together) in the target year to yield a final variable.

The compound projection method was adopted in the OECD's manpower requirements approach to educational planning [417] as originally advocated by Parnes [430]. Other examples appear spasmodically throughout the literature, as do the main criticisms of the approach: first, that planning is often meant to re-orientate the economy off its present trend, and trend estimates of the future should not be in a plan; and, second, one often wants to understand the reasons for the movements of any variable, instead of relating it to the passage of time. Both these needs, the approach, by definition, fails to satisfy.

(b) *Cross-section comparisons.* This technique is imitative, in the sense that it assumes the employment pattern of a country will become that of a more developed one, when it catches up with the latter along the growth path. An extensive set of data for the adoption of this approach is presented by Horowitz, Zymelman and Herrnstadt [251]. A similar advocacy of the approach is made by Farrag [173]; and by Layard and Saigal [322], who also with Emmerij and Thias [167] and Leicester [331] attempt to add explanatory variables to their analysis of differences in international employment pattern.

(c) *Survey questionnaires.* In response to an inquiry, individiual estimates are made by different sectors of the economy, and their figures pooled by a central agency. Consistent categories of manpower and assumptions about the future used by all sectors are crucial to this technique. Despite these hazards, extensive use has been made of the approach: examples are [594, 597, 599].

(d) *Models.* An introduction to model-building is given by Beach [39] and a more comprehensive treatment is provided, for example, by Malinvaud [356]. These techniques allow both a projection of the economic system and a way of linking the future production level with the pattern of manpower required: either ingredient may be simple or sophisticated. An extremely crude link between the economic and manpower variables is suggested by Harbison and Myers [226, 227], and a more detailed one by Tinbergen [571], whose model found application to a number of countries, as described in [572]. Examples of both an advanced economic model and accompanying manpower demand function have been tested in the U.S.A. [648] and the U.K. [334, 545]. The use of such macro-economic models allows a simulation of the economy along paths not implied by past trends alone, and further applies a consistent set of assumptions to all sectors. Accordingly, it is likely that use of this approach will expand in the future, so it may be worthwhile considering the problems that remain in developing the most important equation in the system: a workable manpower function.

The first problem is the forecasting of technological progress, and an understanding of its impact on occupational structure. Jantsch [275] presents an extensive and extremely useful survey of the recently developed techniques of technological forecasting; but these normally handle specific innovations, date their arrival somewhat imperfectly, and are essentially qualitative in the indications they give of their impact on employment patterns. Haase [222], however, shows how their impact on the job structure can be determined at least ten years ahead. An exercise indicating their influence in determining the growth of selected professional occupations over a thirty-year horizon is presented by Leicester [332]. The point made by both Lynn [353] and Mansfield [361] is that the present innovations affecting future technologies are already known. Lave [320] on the other hand has made a summary of techniques that could quantify the pace and direction of technical change, without identifying its type. Given such a situation at present, two proposals have been made. The first, by Crossman [136], is for more detailed studies at the plant or factory level in order to put together a viable theory of the impact of technology on occupational structure. Sokol [525] gives the empirical results of one such case-study. Other results described by Clague [111], Francis [188], Greenberg [217] and Schonning [494] who turn their attention to the most dramatic form of technical change, namely automation; similar studies can be found in [262, 532, 656]. The second proposal is to build into systematic forecasts judgements, based on discussion with the firms in different industrial sectors, of the nature of the impact of technology on manpower: an excellent and detailed example of this combination of qualitative and quantitative techniques is [649]. The use of judgement is better than nothing, but for various reasons we should hope that some viable theory does develop in the future: not only to make such calculations, but to allow feed-back from them. Not only might we wish to know the changes in job patterns due to the existing rate of innovation, but also to know what technological progress should be achieved in order to produce given occupational patterns.

A desired acceleration of technical progress also has planning implications: for the growth, say, in expenditure on research and development.

Meanwhile, it is encouraging to notice that analysis of occupational patterns in their own right has a momentum of its own. In a disaggregated form, this has been done by Knight [302], Meltz [380], Routh [482], Scoville [497] and government departments in the U.K. [627] and U.S.A. [485]. In a weighted, aggregated form—e.g. in an index of the quality of the labour force—this has yielded interesting results in the analyses of Raimon and Stoikov [543], Raimon [466] and Stoikov [542]. It is also encouraging to find analysis of the determinants of productivity change in both the short- and long-run, e.g. in Britain [27, 79, 400], America [164, 253, 293, 312] and other countries [157].

The second major question, raised in the use of models, is the role of factors—other than output and technology—that may determine employment patterns. One such factor is capital used in production. The conventional method of bringing capital into the picture is the production function of economic theory, the present state of which is covered in Brown [83]. O'Herlighy advocates its use [422], while Tinbergen [573] is pessimistic about its immediate applicability. It should be noted that such production functions are supply relationships. A demand system for both capital and labour, which avoids the use of the conventional supply approach, is suggested by Leicester [333].

Another factor missing from most manpower demand analyses —as Hollister [248] and Vaizey [660] point out—is the effect of the supply characteristics of the labour force on the number employed in various occupations. While the omission is generally acknowledged, few attempts to incorporate it have appeared to date: the study by Blank and Stigler [62] and Meltz [380] are among the exceptions, incorporating explicit recognition of the labour market, while Leicester [331] found educational qualification a significant explanatory (supply) variable of the number employed.

The third major issue in such models is the taxonomy of occupations. In most of the applications surveyed, the classifications used have been of an *ad hoc* nature, dictated perhaps by the available data. Alternatively, since manpower forecasts were generally made for the purpose of drawing up educational plans, this tended to result in attempts to shuffle the labour force into categories that are in line with educational indicators of attainment: examples are Parnes [430] and Leicester [330]. A further principle has however been suggested: namely, that the labour force be first disaggregated into functional categories, which may then be further divided into levels of skill. The first idea is suggested by Leicester [333] and an example of such a dual taxonomy illustrated by Scoville [497]. Cain, Hansen and Weisbrod [94] have other ideas on the matter.

(ii) **Occupational vs. educational demands.** This problem lies outside the use of specific techniques of projection, and arises as follows: in quite a few of the exercises referred to above, the demand for manpower is calculated directly in categories of education and training. These have immediate use in educational planning. Some people have, however, recommended a two stage process: calculating occupational demands, and then translating them into educational demands. The activity initiated by Parnes [430] followed this approach, and various independent voices, such as that of Doos [145], insist that employment demands can only have meaning, expressed in occupational terms. The two-stage approach, however, raises a problem of its own: namely, how does one calculate normal or optimum educational and training qualifications for each occupation? Parnes [431] and Folger and Nam [185] have analysed the data for formal education qualifications, and Blum [66] has done the same for informal training. Their conclusion is discouraging. If the past is anything to go by, then people with a wide range of qualifications enter practically every occupation: there is no unique norm for any. Vimont [664] attempts to explain the occupation-education non-concordance; and both O'Donoghue [409] and Sokol [525] offer pragmatic solutions in a planning context. Basically, however, the problem remains unresolved.

(iii) **Other uses of manpower projections.** Most of the manpower forecasts have been made for the purposes of educational planning. For a long while now, however, these have also been used for vocational guidance in the U.S.A. [653], by applying quantitative techniques to a 10-year time horizon; Goldstein [205] found they gave good indications of growing and declining occupations. Leicester, in the U.K., has used quantitative techniques over the same interval for scientific and technological qualifications [328] and qualitative techniques over a longer span of time for careers in important and expanding professions [332]. Ruiter [484] explains why this tends to be the main use of manpower projections in the Netherlands.

(iv) **Specific manpower forecasts.** While it is generally assumed that the total employment pattern should be projected into the future, occasion has sometimes demanded concern with specific manpower types in isolation. In such exercises, scientists and engineers have been the most popular subject [143, 207, 421, 594, 647, 658, 659]. Isolated forecasts have also been made for teachers [593] and for medical [640] and office staff [626]. These exercises have a limited use and validity, because they ignore what else is happening in other forms of employment.

4 THE PROJECTION OF MANPOWER AVAILABILITIES

By comparison, the problem of forecasting the labour that will be available—by type and by number—at some specified date in the future has received scant attention. Population projections are an essential first step [3, 4, 55, 147]; future estimates of the labour force have then to be made [122, 141, 620, 664, 697], usually paying regard to participation and activity rates. This is sometimes disaggregated into occupational categories for the whole of the active population [214]. Similar projections have also been attempted for specific manpower groups, notably for scientists and technologists [207, 594, 658]. A survey of a wide range of existing techniques is given in Johnston [285].

It is worth noting that a radical change would come about in these methods if a single event were to take place: the collection of new flow data within a framework of demographic accounts. Given this, we would know in detail how—between specified dates—people moved from birth through households into schools, from there to employment or higher education, and perhaps back from employment into training; the rates of emigration and immigration; the rates of mortality and retirement; and all this would be detailed in a large number of categories.

What this would make possible is indicated in a general treatment by Stone [547]. The total population at all of a successive series of future dates, divided into active and inactive, between education and staying at home, could be calculated— provided we also knew the transition coefficients indicated by

B

the above data and the pattern of future births. We could go further by making births endogeneous to the growth of the female half of the population; and further still by allowing the transition coefficients to change, either systematically through time or because of explanatory variables suggested by a thorough analysis of such demographic data. This is, if you like, developing *in extenso*, the simple methods already used for population and labour force projections.

In fact, the use of such transition models has already been mooted, and in some cases attempted, by educational planners to monitor the future evolution of schools and higher education; and this is for the simple reason that this is one part of the demographic accounts for which the flows are already quite well documented. Some examples of these models are described in [419, 546]. Projects already exist to extend and expand the use of this approach in the near future. If they succeeed then discerning a gap between future manpower needs and availabilities —for the additional expansion of the education and training system—would be facilitated.

5 THE ANALYSIS OF MANPOWER UTILISATION

For present purposes, misutilisation is defined as either employing more labour than the economy needs, or employing less than the number of people who would like to be gainfully employed. At one and the same, accordingly, employment figures could disregard the well-known phenomena of under-employment and hidden unemployment. Demand for and supply of labour are not in equilibrium; and statistics of employment represent neither the one nor the other.

The question of past misutilisation of manpower cannot be ignored by the manpower planner. Broadly speaking, this is simply because if past data embodied a systematic growing misuse of labour, projecting such data into the future over-states the real needs of the economy; if past measures of the active population exclude hidden unemployment, then simply extrapolating these under-states the number of people who might want to work in the future.

Such a problem for global manpower resources is analysed by Bowen and Finegan [72], Cain [93], Dernberg and Strand [140, 551] and Tella [561, 562] for the U.S.A., and by the ILO

[259] for a large number of other countries. It is clear, however, that there is a further series of sub-problems for specific occupations in specific industrial sectors. Over-manning here, for example, can result from the long-run effects of restrictive practices and the cyclical attempts of employers to hoard labour. Decent time-series analysis of such problems are lacking. Cross-sectional international studies are also few and far between, though some, like Leicester [331], suggest that over-manning can result from labour being under-qualified, in the education and training sense.

This is clearly a matter that should have urgent attention in the future.

6 THE MONITORING OF LABOUR MOBILITY

Free movement of the labour force—within the three-dimensional space of industries, occupations and qualifications—creates a further problem for the detailed manpower plan. Any one manpower stock in this three-fold classification can be effected by mobility in two ways: a movement out creates a demand, and a movement in is a form of supply. Estimates of both needs and availabilities for the future cannot be accurate without these being taken into account.

Whether they can, will be determined by data and existing knowledge of the causes of such movements; it is interesting to note that most of the proposals made by Swerdloff [557] are that such data and knowledge be improved. Parnes [433] and Smith [523] discuss some of the causes of such movements. An analysis of mobility along all three dimensions is given by Harris and Clausen [230], between occupations by Rogoff [479] and [644], between regions by Ladinsky [315] and between countries by Thomas [565] and [595]. Further extensive studies have been made by the OECD [415] and the ILO [263].

This is also another matter that demands more research in the years to come.

7 THE LINK WITH PLANNING AT THE INDUSTRY LEVEL

It should be noted that a fully comprehensive manpower plan for an economy provides some of the inputs for the calculations

made by an industry. These are, among many others, the level
of employment in each industry: on the one hand, in total, and
on the other sub-divided into occupations and qualifications.
Estimates of mobility among industries of those already employed
would be accompanied by figures of those who enter the labour
force for the first time, mainly from systems of education and
training, and how they distribute themselves among industrial
work-places.

Providing, that is, the global planning of manpower resources
is done in sufficient industrial detail, it provides a link with
planning at the industry level. The exchange of information is,
of course, two-way. The plan of any one industry has to fit into
the global picture; and parts of the global picture may be
amended by the improved calculations made by industries.

CHAPTER TWO

MANPOWER PLANNING AT INDUSTRY LEVEL

G. A. Yewdall

Manpower Planning on an industry-wide basis naturally falls between the two levels of national planning and company planning. At the one level it is faced by very similar problems of central planning to those explored in Chapter One. At the other level it impinges upon the local issues discussed in Chapter Three since it is a multitude of company problems that provides the total picture for the industry: the sum of the parts provides the whole.

The natural point of reference for industry-wide planning is to begin with industrial and occupational classifications and definitions [585, 616] before moving into the realms of census data [617, 618] for the broad statistical background. Official sources provide the data to cover working manpower [584, 606, 607] its output [581, 582, 584, 586] and its education and training [641, 642, 602, 604, 605, 611]. In this way the research is able to move from the general to the particular and to obtain broad information about the Industry and its manpower which is selected for particular attention.

Having developed this suitable framework for manpower accounting and having identified, through it, the level of each type of stock and the trends therein, more detailed studies of future needs are called for. The urgency of the need for manpower forecasting on an industry-wide basis was discussed by the Estimates Committee of the House of Commons [615] whose Recommendation No. 7 concluded that:

'The Manpower Research Unit of the Ministry of Labour should carry out a comprehensive assessment of the future manpower needs of every industry with a view to establishing the way in which retraining can contribute to an effective redeployment of labour.'

The Manpower Research Unit of the Department of Employment and Productivity was created specifically to deal with this type of exercise mentioned above. It has produced several studies on particular aspects both of occupational manpower and of specific industries [620–626]. These studies are of special relevance to central economic planning within the National Economic Development Councils, to the planning of training within the Industrial Training Boards, and to individual firms within the particular industries. If more information is required than that provided from these studies, then investigations may be made in greater depth of particular industries or occupational groups [630, 636]. Regularly collected statistics are supplemented by special surveys and questionnaires; and they may be used for comparative studies between and within industries, regions and occupations.

Comparable overseas studies are given by [644, 645, 647–650]; and by [652], dealing with the telephone industry; [651], with the Health Service; [646] with Civil Aviation.

A considerable body of literature on human development is now being built up from the publications of the Industrial Training Boards. Their standards for training and development have helped firms to improve manpower utilization and introduce better career planning. These standards are well illustrated in the examples of training recommendations on management, on supervisors, and professional engineers, in the publications of one of the Industrial Training Boards, that for the Engineering Industry [609–614].

Special attention has been devoted to scientific and technological manpower. Information is available on their calibre [257, 603] in addition to studies in depth of their migration, supply and demand [595, 596, 600]. One would expect that similar studies of non-scientific and non-technological manpower would be produced in the future because planning is a total exercise. It is necessary to know what experience and expertise a job requires as distinct from the experience and expertise of the person who is performing the job. Only by completing this exercise in full is it possible to decide which types of people are economically more apt for which jobs.

Having obtained data, it is necessary to organize it in a meaningful way. This has been done in considerable detail for the Iron and Steel Industry, where a variety of methods or 'models' have been developed and their use explored to make alternative estimates of future manning and training loads [58, 59]. Unless the manpower situation is relatively simple, with established manning scales related to variations in production, simple indicators are unlikely to prove useful for forecasting; rather it is necessary to take into account several factors simultaneously and evaluate the effect of each. Even then, uncertainties of data, variations in utilization, inconsistencies in classification, incomplete knowledge of the supply position, all mean that it is unwise to have much faith in a forecast based on a single set of assumptions or a single approach. It is often better to explore a whole range of different forecasts. This offsets the fact that often there is not sufficient data or experience to be sure of the best representation of the behaviour being forecast. In particular any forecasting system must be flexible, so that specific knowledge or expert opinion regarding some aspect of the forecasts can be readily taken into account. At the same time it is desirable to build a 'model' or mathematical representation of the relationship implied by the forecasts even though some of the figures will be subjective. The availability of a model or set of models enables the forecaster to examine the consequences of alternative assumptions regarding the economic environment, government policy, labour productivity agreements and so on.

These models are usually classified as 'econometric', in which the level of manpower is related statistically to the values of various other factors such as investment, plant, production level, unemployment or Gross National Product. In other words the relationships are not necessarily exact but are reasonable approximations to describe the functioning of the manpower system under study. Such models, which generally need to be explored by computer, can provide a ready means of examining alternative assumptions. Econometric models form the conceptual framework for much of the national economic planning being done at present. They have been applied to manpower at national level both in the UK and the US [334, 648].

A popular type of econometric model, which is relatively simple to construct and manipulate, is the input-output model. There is a simplified introduction to input-output models in Redfern [468]: while their application to inter-industry mobility of labour is illustrated by studies in the electronics industry [636].

Forecasting can be done efficiently only if the end use of the forecast is clearly understood. In general the forecast is a part of a planning exercise to ensure the proper supply and deployment of manpower in the future. It may be that the best disposition of manpower in an industry will not be in accord with the requirements or expectations of particular companies or occupational groups. If a forecast for an industry is not to prove naive, it must consequently take into account the effect of the varying pressures in the industry for a continuing or a greater share of the total resources. Many attempts at forecasting industry requirements for manpower have failed either because an equalization of pressures has been assumed when calculating the whole or because forecasts of individual companies have been summed to arrive at the whole. Clearly those two approaches must be reconciled and the importance of continued consultation cannot be overstressed. Also important is the need for thorough understanding of the nature of an industry's utilization of its manpower. Historical numbers are not sufficient. The forecaster needs to be acquainted with the particular, often unique, changes which are occurring in the industry, both in terms of technology and of job-men effectiveness.

Studies in job-men effectiveness are generally seen in terms of output, productivity and the contribution made by different quantities and qualities of manpower. The starting point for such industry-broad financial studies is the national income accounts [586–7] while the more restricted pay-off measurements are discussed in [51, 64]. These manpower investment studies of the concept of human capital overlap with cost-benefit analysis [63, 454] and it becomes difficult to distinguish what changes are taking place (and ought to take place). This is not only because there is a lack of data, but also because there is a lack of agreement as to how the data should be interpreted.

At the company level the position is slightly less acute. There may be agreed business plans and corporate objectives [15, 224] which heavily depend upon technological forecasting [275] for estimating the correct manning loads and utilization factors in planning manpower requirements. But studies of value-added and productivity bargaining lead into the difficult areas of measuring human motivation and offering incentives, which depend upon the particular circumstances [238, 376].

At this level there is more concern with individual career

development than with issues which can be regarded as industry-wide manpower budgeting: the problems are best approached through specific limited studies since industry-wide generalizations are difficult to make. Appropriate general introductions to the planning of company manpower resources are given by [352, 608, 634, 638].

CHAPTER THREE

MANPOWER PLANNING AT THE LEVEL OF THE FIRM

D. J. Bell, W. R. Hawes, C. G. Lewis, C. J. Purkiss

1 INTRODUCTION

Manpower is a scarce resource. As such it must be planned and controlled in the same way as other resources. Manpower planning, therefore, has links with, and interacts with, the other planning activities of management. Planning is discussed in these general terms by Dale [138], and Ansoff [13]. Case studies of planning, including several concerned with manpower, are given in Steiner [535–539]. Other references are Branch [75–76], and the Irish Management Institute [271].

The need to ensure that future labour requirements will be available, and to increase the organisation's productivity, are two important reasons for undertaking manpower planning. Shortages of certain grades of manpower have given recruitment plans and training plans critical importance in many organisations. On the other hand, pressures to increase productivity have brought about reductions in staff, making it essential to plan to handle, or, if possible, to avoid, a redundancy programme.

Productivity bargaining demands planning, to clarify management's aims; consequently forecasting methods may be necessary to measure the effectiveness of the agreement. A longer term benefit may be the trust built up when it is seen that management, as a matter of course, examines the implications for manpower of its future actions. Also, career planning and management development schemes are a part of the overall manpower plan.

The reasons for undertaking manpower studies are examined in detail by the Edinburgh Group [292], and the Department of Employment and Productivity booklet [608]. The basis of manpower forecasts must be the overall company plans, incorporating production, technological innovation, group development, marketing policy, and financial plans, or their equivalent in service industries. Without knowing the objectives of the organisation, the manpower planner will be operating in a vacuum and will be able neither to produce a meaningful manpower plan nor to set his own priorities and objectives for carrying out his task in the most efficient way.

Manpower Planning in the organisation has two main stages:

(i) The forecast of manpower requirements, sometimes called the 'demand forecast'—how many men, in terms of the approximate number of posts, will be required, in suitable categories of manpower and at suitable intervals of time in the future. This is treated in Section Two of this Chapter.

(ii) Where the men to fill these posts are to come from, often called the 'Manpower Plan proper'. This stage is, in turn, broken into two parts: the internal supply forecast —how many of the present staff will remain at the date being considered in the future, assuming no other action is taken—the External supply forecast—what the state of the labour market is likely to be.

The internal supply in the future can, of course, be affected by managerial action, but the external supply cannot easily be altered by one organisation alone. However, one part of the planning activity which affects both is the training plan, which may alter the internal structure by, for example, retraining existing staff, or may take in new staff and then train them, as in the case of apprentices.

Finally, there is the constant feedback from the results of the planning stage to earlier stages or even to the objectives of the organisation. The manpower supply has to match the manpower requirements. This can be done by changing the supply through managerial actions, such as increasing the amount of training being done, or by changing the manpower requirements as, for example, by plans to increase the company's productivity. There can also be a feedback to the company objectives, either when the manpower plan shows that they are unattainable through manpower shortage or when the manpower planning process is being used to test the likely effect of different decisions which management could take.

The whole framework of manpower planning is set out in the Edinburgh Group Report [292] already mentioned, as well as the

DEP book [608]. Lynch [352] also develops the same theme. These three books all investigate some of the techniques involved in carrying this process through, and the Edinburgh Group report discusses some implications to the Government arising from needs of companies in manpower planning. The Manpower Research Unit's report [608] is addressed to managers. It is well laid out, and has a good bibliography. Lynch looks at much the same topic, and contains more case studies, but no bibliography, and with little attention to the difficulties involved. The Edinburgh Group Report contains a discussion of company manpower planning—in particular the decisions to be made and difficulties to be overcome, and comes up with some interesting recommendations. Many of the personnel techniques associated with manpower planning are dealt with by McBeath [372].

The bases of the forecast of requirements are the company's plans. The starting point for the forecast, however, is a thorough analysis of the present manpower, a 'Manpower Inventory', for which sound personnel records are needed—see Durham [161], and Buzzard and Radforth [92]. A good study of computerised records, which can provide a powerful aid to manpower planning, is given by Wille [690]. Increases in manpower productivity, whether from technological improvements, or genuine improvements in manpower utilisation, will also need to be built into the forecast, and these will be based on improvements shown in the past, together with an estimation of their economic advantages. Improvements may also be made from an examination of what might be happening in other firms with the same problems. Further improvements may be found necessary when the supply of manpower is examined, and this is one example of the constant interactions between one part of the plan and another, as well as between the manpower and other business plans—see Section 4.

The forecast of internal supply is a question of predicting the survival of staff. This is dealt with more fully in Section 5, but two useful summaries of work in this field are given by Bryant [88] and Chaplin [109]. At some levels of manpower, this will also involve career planning, as, for example, set out by Young [702].

The training plan is one way within the organisation's control to supply manpower in the future. In Britain this also involves government, through the Industrial Training Act, the effect of which is discussed by Page [429]. The involvement of the Training Boards set up under the Act in manpower planning is discussed both in the Edinburgh Group Report [292], and in Bell and Coleman [46, 47]. The Carr report [619], in discussing training, gave a very perceptive summary of what is involved in manpower planning in 1958; the same points have been re-iterated by the Central Training Council [588–590].

The forecast of external supply available to a particular organisation depends on forecasts of the workforce and also on the likely share of this supply; this in turn, especially in the case of larger firms, implies overall demand forecasts. Forecasts of the workforce as a whole are dealt with in the first report of the Manpower Research Unit [620], but little is available in the way of forecasts of particular types of manpower or of the overall demand. The official statistics available in Britain are given in an appendix to [608], and will be found here between [581–630]. They are discussed by Crossley [134, 135]. However, these are virtually all historical data, and a great deal of work needs to be done in this field. The manpower planner at present is in the position of having to make his own projections.

Government may also be involved in activities directly affecting manpower supply in the organisation; [556] and [165] give the situation in Sweden and Ireland, in both of which countries considerable thought has been given to this subject.

The place of manpower planning in the organisation, whether it should be linked with the personnel function or with the other corporate planning activities, is examined, in the light of US experience, by Geisler [198]. Wherever it is carried out within the organisation, it is clear that manpower planning is a part of the overall management function of planning. The forecasts made are dependent on management decisions on objectives and policy, and form an aid to decision by management on future action. They are made for management to change them rather than as a pre-diction of an unalterable future. The types of forecast which can be made and the way in which they aid decisions are discussed by Bell [45].

Manpower planning in the organisation can, therefore, be defined as the systematic analysis of the company's manpower resources, the construction of a forecast of its future manpower requirements from this base, with special concentration on efficient manpower utilisation at both these stages and the planning necessary to ensure that the manpower supply will match the forecast requirements. The planning stage depends on the forecasts of the supply of manpower from within and without and embraces recruitment, career and training plans.

2 THE ESTIMATION OF FUTURE REQUIREMENTS OF MANPOWER

This Section deals with the forecasting activity itself. Questions of manpower needs, which involve wider considerations of labour utilisation, are thus outside its scope. It is sufficient to note on this point that there is little purpose in projecting manning standards without taking into account possible improvements in labour utilisation to existing methods of work.

Methods of forecasting future manpower requirements can be divided broadly into four types: Predictions based on management intuition unbacked by statistical analysis, those made with the aid of various statistical techniques, those based on the use of work study measurements, and those based on measures of productivity. A general discussion of these is to be found in [608], and other works such as the Edinburgh Group [292], Lynch [352], Geisler [198], McBeath [372], and Hinrichs [245] are also helpful in setting the background to the manpower forecasting process and in introducing a variety of forecasting methods.

In all such approaches, some attempt must be made to relate manpower requirements to expected future levels of production output, sales, costs, and so on. It follows that an essential prerequisite to the manpower planning and forecasting process is a close knowledge of the company's objectives on these wider fronts. Manpower planning should thus be seen as one part of the process of overall corporate planning, which was discussed in general terms in the previous section. Jantsch [275] deals at considerable length with the problems encountered in long term forecasting of technological change, and provides a useful bibliography on this topic.

Little published material is available on the extent of manpower forecasting in British Industry, although a study by the DEP's Manpower Research Unit [620] contains a comment on the situation in 1964. For North America, Ferber [175] is relevant. A number of generally useful case studies which give considerable insight into the manpower forecasting (and planning) process in firms have, however, been published. Barkin [29] presents a series of general studies prepared for the

OECD, which were later summarised and evaluated by Wedderburn [677]. This last presents a useful account of adjustment procedures and the organisation of manpower planning in the face of technological change. Beaumont and Helfgott [40] contains a section (pp. 266–274) dealing with the experiences of a number of companies in manpower planning. Blaug, Peston, and Ziderman [64] is an account of a preliminary study on the utilisation of qualified manpower in electrical engineering firms and it contains a number of hints to the intending manpower planner in a large firm. Kuhn [313], although not dealing explicitly with the manpower forecasting process, makes some useful points on the difficulties of planning future manpower levels with the introduction of an entirely new technology.

On the forecasting activities of particular firms, a number of studies are available. Barkin [29] has already been mentioned. Papers by Chadwick, and his associates [80] and [105] deal with the work of the British Petroleum Company. Hodgson [247], discusses manpower forecasting in the Ford Motor Company, Pelling [443] supplements the description of the manpower planning work of the National Coal Board contained in Barkin [29] and Wedderburn [677]. Smith [516–519] discusses in some detail the manpower forecasting carried out for the Royal Navy. A report from the OECD [416] on personnel planning in firms describes the impression gained by a German team which visited several British firms who had shown an interest in the problems of manpower planning. Farrimond [174] describes in general terms manpower planning in Imperial Metal Industries Ltd., and finally Prybylski [458] deals with manpower planning in Trans-World Airlines.

It is clear that worthwhile manpower forecasting will be possible only if adequate personnel statistics are available. This has been stressed in Section 1, and the books by Durham [161], and Wille [690] already recommended. A useful pamphlet from the National Institute of Industrial Psychology [92] gives a good indication of what may happen when there are inadequate personnel statistical records.

Much remains to be done on particular methods of forecasting manpower requirements. At present little detailed work has been published, although many of the statistical techniques employed by sales forecasters are directly relevant—Coutie and others [127]. Kendall [294, 295] gives a good description of various statistical approaches, whilst practical examples of the use of regression analysis can be found in Drui [151] and Gascoigne [194]. A bibliography of elementary statistical techniques is contained in [608].

In forecasting methods which explicitly use a measure of labour productivity, future manpower requirements are derived from planned future output or sales levels, and measures of future productivity levels—broadly defined as labour input per unit of output. The difficulties of measurement in this field are well known. A useful survey is that by Easterfield [163], and Navas [399] and Ewing [171–172] provide hints on the ways in which measures of productivity can be turned to use in company manpower forecasting.

3 THE EXTERNAL SUPPLY FORECAST

Planning and research work on the external supply of manpower can be regarded as falling into two parts:

(i) at Company and Local level;
(ii) at Regional level.

The main need for the company manpower planner is to know the local availability of manpower by type of skill, age, etc., and, if possible, how much he is likely to get, for some time ahead. For this he might consult the local offices of the Department of Employment and Productivity. Data from local schools, and figures from the Youth Employment Service all help, but there are very few standard publications to aid him. At National Level, the outflow of highly qualified men from Universities, Technical Colleges, etc., is available to firms from the publications of the University Grants Committee [641–643]. The outflow from schools and universities is also obtained from the Department of Education [602–605], but a company manpower planner trying to forecast local supply of a particular skill in a particular future year has a difficult job on his hands. Those who do best are situated in one of the regions where groups of company planners, university and research departments, have joined together to investigate future supply and demand of manpower, broken down in great detail over the next five to ten years.

An example of this type of co-operation is the study by the University of Hull into the Humberside region. In collaboration with local companies they are looking in the short term up to 1971, and in the longer term up to 1981. They will produce a detailed labour supply forecast for differing skills for the area around Hull. Another example of co-operation is the setting up, by the Manchester Group of the Operational Research Society Manpower Planning Study Group, of 'town meetings'—in which members who all live in the same town, but of different firms, professions, etc., will meet regularly to discuss common manpower problems, and how best to solve them.

At the London School of Economics, the Unit for Economic and Statistical Studies on Higher Education has a long-term study into several aspects of manpower work. Their first aim is to improve the methods of estimating manpower needs, but they are also assessing the current national position as to whether men are being given an education fitting them to the job that they will take. Another part of their work concerns a study to see how the manpower supply is related to the financial rewards in the particular field. This work follows on from the study on the relation between age, education, training-on-the-job, and occupational development in industry. The works of Blaug [63–65] are good reading on this topic.

Availability research in the Scientific, Engineering, and Technological field is carried out at the Ministry of Technology [630]. They have held triennial surveys of qualified manpower in this field [597–599]. They also try to find out the job actually done by qualified men in the scientific field, which is often far removed from jobs suited to them by their qualifications. The Department of Education and Science approaches the problem by the construction of educational models, and the use of techniques such as input-output analysis [468]. The same topic is pursued in Alper [6], using the concept of a bottleneck, where too many people are trying to get into a particular occupation or university. Wider models have been produced by Darmstadter [139], Dill [144], and Grais [214].

Abroad, a great deal of work is done for research organisations, often financed or helped by the Government. Typical of their publications are those of the George Washington University for the US Navy, the Rand Corporation, or the Army Personnel Research Office. Most of these reports are based on national considerations [645–659]; it would seem that reports on local topics get little circulation.

4 THE ANALYSIS OF MANPOWER UTILISATION

Improvements in the productivity of manpower are clearly important in their own right. They are also important as an integral part of the manpower requirements forecast because:

(i) the requirements forecast should have a sound base, so that any current misuse of manpower is not carried into the future;

(ii) improvements in productivity will continue to be achieved in the future; a forecast of them must, therefore, be made and incorporated into the forecast of requirements.

Such improvements in productivity are frequently achieved through technological advance, and these need to be distinguished from improvements which result from better management, better organisation, and better worker co-operation. Terminology used in the literature varies, but it is convenient to use productivity as the generic term, under which are subsumed technological change and manpower utilisation, restricting this last term to improvements in the use of manpower not resulting from new machinery or equipment.

Improvements through technological change have received considerable attention, for example, Barkin [29], Wedderburn [677], the European Productivity Agency [170] and Salter [490]. A unified treatment of improved manpower utilisation has not been made, however, except in general, exhortatory publications, such as that of the UK Ministry of Labour [629]. In fact, the methods of improving utilisation are a collection of management techniques and practices, which may be useful severally or in combination according to the circumstances of the organisation.

Foremost among the techniques is Work Study, the basis of which is well described by Currie [137]. Cost-Benefit Analysis can also result in improvements—see Prest and Turvey [454]. The allocation of manpower resources can be greatly improved by the use of the Critical Path Method (C.P.M.), or related techniques; an introduction to this is provided by Lockyer [348], Baker and Evis [25], and Shaffer, Ritter and Hayer [501].

Amongst the management practices, the one on which emphasis is placed at the moment is productivity bargaining, which is introduced in the case study of the British prototype agreement at the Fawley Refinery by Flanders [182], and is examined by the Institute of Personnel Management [231]. Productivity bargaining seeks to buy out restrictive practices and secure the workers' co-operation in exchange, but it also imposes a discipline on managers to organise work appropriately. A practice which puts the onus for improvement on the manager is management by objectives, an outline of which is given by Humble [254]. This is a system of management for the organisation as a whole, but it does involve the appraisal of individual's performance and thus links with staff appraisal schemes, which are dealt with by Tiffin and McCormick [569], and Whisler and Harper [681]. Some special points on appraisal are made by McGregor [378], Rowe [483], and Stewart [540]. Appraisal of performance leads to management development, which naturally aims, though in somewhat general terms, to improved managerial performance, and thus productivity. Roberts [475] is a useful introduction to this subject, and the Central Training Council also discusses it [590].

On the other hand, the onus can be placed on the worker through incentive payment schemes—see Marriott [365]. These schemes are, however, somewhat unpredictable in their effect: see Lupton [349] for an analysis of them, and Brown [85] for a study of one case when incentives failed. The UK National Board for Prices and Incomes has also provided a useful report [632]. Motivation to work can also be affected by other means than money. The study of human motivation is a subject in itself, but an indication of the problems and theories can be obtained from the work of Vroom [665]. Some of the earliest work in this field—the Hawthorne experiments—is described by Mayo whose books [370, 371] remain important to the subject. Another relevant book is Herzberg [238].

Measurement of productivity within an organisation can help the manager by revealing changes over time and drawing parallels with other organisations. However, measurement is a complex matter. Indices are only partial indicators of good performance, particularly in international comparisons, since there are normally other factors, such as differing labour costs, which make the best conjunction of resources different from one country to another. Measures are dealt with by Easterfield [163], Bartholomew [31], Kendrick and Creamer [296], and the OECD [410]. An index which makes adjustments for the

variables which otherwise make comparisons incomplete has
been devised by Electricité de France [166]. Such an index is
useful for measuring real progress over time. Partial indices do,
however, have their uses. Examination of the performance of
other companies does indicate what can be achieved, but not
what is desirable. Another technique, activity sampling, may also
be useful in revealing the present level of utilisation. This is set
out by Heiland and Richardson [240], and, in a variant form,
by Wirdenius [687].

Measures of productivity normally demonstrate the utilisation
of industrial staff. However, highly trained staff are frequently
misused, as is documented by Pym [461]. The importance of
educated manpower in industry is examined by Blaug, Peston,
and Ziderman [64], whose book introduces the study currently
conducted by the Industrial Manpower Project at the London
School of Economics.

In making his forecast of manpower requirements, the manpower planner needs measures of productivity in the past as a
basis for estimating the rate of improvement in the future; he
also needs to know management's objectives as far as productivity
is concerned. He must then modify his forecast to allow for this;
this problem is examined in the Manpower Research Unit
Report [608]. Improvements from technological change may,
according to some techniques, be incorporated into the forecast
automatically if, for example, the forecast is derived from
manning schedules relating to new plant. However, if the technique is to predict according to past relationships between
production and manpower, perhaps using multiple regression,
technological change, as well as improved manpower utilisation
must be estimated separately. The method will often be an
intuitive one, a compound of past performance and management objectives, although it may be aided occasionally by more
scientific methods. For example, the 'learning curve' predicts
the rate at which staff learn a new process and thus affects the
rate of increase in productivity—see Broster [81] and Simone
[509].

Forecasts of requirements can be modified for improved
productivity, and these modifications will be based on economically justified improvements. However, when the forecast has
been drawn up and an attempt made to match it to the forecast
of manpower supply, it may be that a future shortage of man-

power, possibly in certain categories, is indicated. There may be several solutions to this problem, such as retraining, but one solution is improved utilisation. In this way there is a 'feed-back' from the planning stage, which involves changes in the requirement forecasts and thus in the plans for meeting these requirements. The justification for this is then less clearly economic, but it is rather the shortage reason for improvement. However, it is still making the best use of resources available. There is a need for a book dealing with this aspect of manpower planning.

The achievement of changes in manpower utilisation can well stem directly from the manpower planning activity. The whole process of planning should, through concentrating management attention on the appropriate problems, achieve an improvement in manpower utilisation. The scrutiny of top management, whether or not they decide on any manpower controls, can have a salutary effect. Manpower budgets, which are a form of short-term forecast, are normally linked with controls, and the examination of manpower requirements alongside marketing, production, and financial plans can prompt improvement—as is shown in Walker [668].

The achievement of changes incorporated into the manpower forecast may also depend on the successful carrying through of the manpower plan. In particular, the training plan may be crucial, if retraining or improved performance is involved—see Borenschot [53]. It may also depend on mobility of staff, between places and occupations; the national situation dealt with in Chapter One has implications within the organisation on mobility and the influence exerted by the organisation through pay differentials has been examined by the OECD [415].

Finally achievement depends on the management of the changes themselves. Redundancies and redeployment of labour are matters of industrial relations and, as such, are not fully covered in this bibliography, but some of the effects of change on people are given in Barkin [29].

5 THE FLOW OF PERSONNEL

The first part of this section describes the statistics, etc., needed before the flow of manpower into, within, and out of a company can be measured, and analysed. Then three aspects of the flow of manpower are treated in more detail; they are:

Recruitment and Training;
Career Planning;
Labour Turnover.

Manpower planning at the level of the firm will only be successful if the basic records and statistics of personnel are kept in a comprehensive and up-to-date manner. For larger companies this will usually mean computer records; small firms may have their personnel files on punch cards or keep some central clerical record.

However, it is often the case that manpower planners have low priority on the use of personnel files, even though the company may have the records available, and the ADP potential to extract the statistics. Firstly, the Pay and Accounting departments must be satisfied; then there are the demands of Civil Service departments, such as the Board of Trade and the Department of Employment and Productivity. The statistics collected by these departments are grouped together and published at Industry level, as is shown in Chapter Two.

The Industrial Training Boards, the Economic Development Committees, and the National Board for Prices and Incomes, are all asking for more and more information; Research Units, and sociologists from University Research Departments all increase the demand for output from the personnel files. The effect on ADP staff, already hard-worked, is to cause frustration, and this is well shown in Mumford [393]. The planning that is needed at company level to take into account the computer expansion is discussed in the recent work of Mumford and Ward [394]. The effect on manpower planners is twofold; they either go off and set up statistical personnel record systems of their own, or they resign themselves to the limited data available and make the most of it by inventing complex mathematical models of manpower systems.

Smith [516–519] describes how a statistical record system was set up in the management of Royal Navy manpower, and how forecasting models have used this as raw data. However, there are obvious advantages in keeping one set of records for all purposes as is pointed out by the Edinburgh Group [292]. The compromise that is reached by many organisations, though little is published yet, is the extraction from the main personnel pay and accounting record of a smaller record containing only data needed for manpower planning. This could be done at regular intervals, say weekly, or monthly for each person working in the organisation. The list of data needed in the extract is to be found in many books. Lynch [352 pp. 128–144] has a good summary, and lists some of the problems to be found in practice. It is as well at this point to ensure that the codes and methods of classification are as compatible with other companies, government departments, etc., as possible.

The books that go into the detail of specific aspects of company planner's job are few as yet, and are often slightly academic. This is because the manpower plan of a company is not something that can be said to produce answers, but, like any other planning, it needs constant revision, and the results of today only serve to guide the input for tomorrow. This point is well brought out in Purkiss [459].

Recruitment has been one of the areas of moderate success in the manpower planning field, although many firms still recruit for only one year ahead, without looking at the long-term, say 5–10 years. The obvious solution to the short-term problem may be the wrong one when looked at over a longer period. For example, it may be more profitable to recruit, in the long run, a less intelligent group of people, since those with high intelligence tend to leave after a short time. Jones [288–289], and Smith [517–519] provide examples of models which enable one to calculate the recruitment needed in each particular skill to meet the given future requirement. A realistic model enables one to feed in expected recruitment, and see whether the requirement is met, and, of course, vice versa.

Models of recruitment are closely tied up with models of career planning; this is especially true when the career patterns of the future are being investigated. Some assumption must be made about future patterns of recruitment, or if the model is more complicated, some limiting values or constraints must be placed on the recruitment. There is a fair amount of work being done on the success of recruitment campaigns, and here multivariate techniques are used to isolate factors which may affect the reason why people join a particular firm.

The efficiency of interview methods, selection, and placement procedures is well discussed by Drenth [150], with an extensive bibliography on the topic. The Dutch Defence Ministry have published their scheme for allocating national service personnel by computer; in this, the job in the service is broken down into components, and matched against qualifications and attributes of entrants. Draft cards, training courses, and final postings are produced from an IBM 7094. The American armed forces have produced countless reports on selection procedures and related topics—the works of the Army Personnel Research Office, USA, are good examples [424, 425].

Training has been looked at from many points of view: the psychological, by Annett [11]; military by Wallis [669]; economic by Smith [516]. The last two papers are to be found in the proceedings of a NATO conference [284], which contains a collection of many good papers on several aspects of manpower planning. Training has, in general, been considered in Chapter Two, with reference to the publications of the Industrial Training Boards. Mathematical techniques have also been applied, e.g. Leese [327], which describes an application of dynamic programming methods to the scheduling of training in a large organisation.

Career planning is becoming a factor of greater importance as time goes on. With the tight manpower field that exists today, especially in the highly qualified range, it is essential that the structure of a company is such that the policies of promotion, recruitment, training, and so on, fit into an overall pattern that both keeps the company efficient in the short term, and does not lay down inbalances for the future.

Most of the work being done in this field occurs within the bounds of the single company, or organisation. The manpower planner tries to apply certain techniques in an attempt to find out better ways of ensuring successful careers for the members of his organisation, which remain compatible with the organisation staying efficient. Techniques can range from simple arithmetic analysis of the past data available—Wood [696], to very complex applications of such skills as linear programming [469], in which the individual is treated as if he were part of an inventory problem. The aspect which is difficult to investigate in any of these techniques is the personal one—the qualifications and qualities of the individual men involved.

Literature on career planning is growing, but is not very large at present. All Bartholomew's work is relevant [31–35], and there are several good case studies. The early work of Seal [499], Vajda [661, 662], and Solomon [526] lead on to the use of computers as suggested by Young [702], and Young and Almond [701]. These use Markov Theory to forecast future structures. Gani [193] predicts future distributions of university staff, and other examples of the use of Markov Theory are [363, 460, 703].

The planning of careers in the Armed Forces has come in for a great deal of attention. In this country, the work of Jones [288, 289], and Smith [516–519] in the Royal Navy has been mentioned already. The British Army is experimenting with a stationary state model of trade structures, and with projecting present states into the future using a computer to evaluate different policies. The German Air Force have extended this idea into a projection model using quadratic programming and have published an account of this—Stolley [544]. The Royal Air Force is now studying an application of linear programming to predicting future manpower structures and recruitment needs—a paper on this topic will be given at the NATO conference on Mathematical Models in Manpower Planning, Portugal, 1969, the proceedings of which will be published— Smith [520]. The Canadian Air Forces have made detailed investigations of their manpower systems. Cotterill [126] creates a model for personnel inventory prediction, based on the qualifications of individuals. The US forces have many models, all making extensive use of their computer facilities—Safeer [486, 487] are good examples.

On the company level, career plans can be linked with models of performance appraisal—and works on this topic are Tiffin and McCormick [569], and Whistler and Harper [681].

When a model becomes extensive or involves many iterations, a computer is usually needed, and this restricts planning of this type to companies with access to a fairly fast scientific computer. Most machines have standard programming packages for such techniques as linear and quadratic programming, so the actual computer programming involved in this sort of complex model need not be great. However, the more complex the model, the longer and more expensive it is to run on a computer, and the results may not justify its use. Much of the value of using a computer in this field lies in the ability to simulate future changes of policy by altering one or more parameters of the model; but if the solution to the problem is obvious—i.e., to recruit more men, then the computer will only confirm your thoughts, and cost a lot of money doing it.

One of the very first social processes to be looked at in any detail was that of Labour Turnover. Early work in this field was carried out at the Tavistock Institute in 1950-1952, by Rice, Hill and Trist [470–473]. This was extended by Lane and Andrew [317], and later by Silcock [505]. The cost of Labour Turnover is discussed in many books of the National Economic Development Office [637, 638, 639], while the psychological aspect is well covered in Kriedt and Gadel [311], Tiffin and Phelan [568], and Poidevin [449].

It is now well accepted that the explanation of past Labour Turnover is well approximated by certain mathematical distributions, and the success of past policies can be analysed in this way. However, the forecasting of future turnover is another matter, and a great deal is being done and will continue to be done. The publications of Bartholomew [31–34] again sum up the techniques available, and his latest book [35], which has an excellent bibliography of its own, contains applications of statistics to all areas of manpower planning, particularly recruitment, labour turnover, and grading structures. The treatment requires a high mathematical aptitude to assimilate it, and one may look in vain for a model to meet one's needs exactly. It is an excellent book of ideas.

CHAPTER FOUR

MANPOWER PLANNING
BIBLIOGRAPHY

1 ACKOFF, R.   'Meaning of Strategic Planning.'
                             Management Science, Oct., 1966.
2 ADELMAN, I. G.   'A Stochastic Analysis of the Size Dis-
                             tribution of Firms.'
                             JASA, Vol. 53, pp. 893–904, 1958.
3 ADELMAN, I. G.   'An Econometric Analysis of Popula-
                             tion Growth.'
                             American Economic Review, Vol. 53,
                             No. 3, p. 314, 1963.
4 AKERS, D. S.   'Cohort Fertility versus Parity Pro-
                             gression as Methods of Projecting
                             Births.'
                             Demography, Vol. 2, p. 414, 1965.
5 ALMOND, G. (with   See No. 701
    YOUNG, A.)
6 ALPER, P.   'Educational Models in Manpower
    (ARMITAGE P.,   Planning and Control.'
    and SMITH, C. S.)   *ORQ*, Vol. 16, p. 20, 1967.
7 ALTERMAN, J.   'Inter-Industry Employment Require-
                             ments.'
                             Monthly Labour Review, Vol. 88, No. 7,
                             p. 841, 1965.
8 ANDERSON, R. G.   *Management Strategies.*
                             McGraw-Hill, New York, 1966.
9 ANDERSON, R. G.   *Theoretical Considerations of Educational*
    (and   *Planning.*
    BOWMAN, G.)   Syracuse University, USA, 1964.
10 ANDREW, J. E.   See No. 317.
    (with Lane, K. F.)
11 ANNETTE, J.   'Task Analysis for Training.'
    (and   *Manpower Research in the Defence Context.*

	DUNCAN, K.)	EUP, London, and American Elsevier, New York, 1969.)
12	ANSOFF, H. I.	'Planning as a Practical Management Tool.' *Financial Executive*, June, 1964.
13	ANSOFF, H. I.	*Corporate Strategy.* Penguin Books, London and Baltimore, Md., 1968.
14	ARBONS, A. G.	*Selection for Industrial Leadership.* Oxford University Press, London and New York, 1953.
15	ARGENTI, A. J.	*Corporate Planning—A Practical Guide.* Allen and Unwin, London, 1968.
16	ARGYRIS, C.	'Human Problems with Budgets.' *Harvard Business Review*, Vol. 31, pp. 37–110, 1953.
17	ARMITAGE, P. (with ALPER, P., and SMITH, C. S.)	See No. 6.
18	ARMITAGE, P.	'The Comparison of Survival Curves.' *JRSS Series A*, Vol. 122, pp. 279–300, 1959.
19	ARMSTRONG, D.	*Manpower Planning — Occupations and Talent.* Document T.924, Tavistock Institute, London, 1966.
20	ARMSTRONG, D.	*Manpower Planning and the Industrial Firm.* Document T.1022, Tavistock Institute, London, 1967.
21	ARMSTRONG, D.	*Short Annotated Bibliography.* Document T.934, Tavistock Institute, London, 1967.
22	BACIE	*A Standard Method of Costing the Training of Apprentices* BACIE, London, 1965.
23	BACIE	*Training Manuals for Office Supervisors.* BACIE, London, 1965.
24	BAGCUS, P. M.	'Effects of Leadership Training on the Attitudes and Behaviour of NCO's.' *Manpower Research in the Defence Context.*

EUP, London and American Elsevier, New York, 1969.

25 BAKER, B. N.
(and EVIS, R.)
An Introduction to PERT/CPM.
Irwin, Homewood, Ill., and London, 1964.

26 BALFOUR, A.
NATO Force Planning Cost Model.
Research Publication 5066, Rand Corp. of America, USA, 1965.

27 BALL, R. J. (and ST. CYR, E.)
'Short-term Employment Functions in British Manufacturing Industry.'
Review of Economic Studies, Vol. 33, p. 179, 1966.

28 BANERJEE, R.
(with MISRA, R.)
See No. 384.

29 BARKIN, S. (ed.)
Technical Change and Manpower Planning; Co-ordination at the Enterprise Level.
Manpower and Social Affiairs Directorate, OECD, Paris, 1967.

30 BARRETT, L.
(and LANG, G.)
'Preselection in the Prediction of Job Tenure.'
Journal of Industrial Psychology, Vol. 1, p. 1, 1963.

31 BARTHOLOMEW, D. J.
'Note on the Measurement and Prediction of Labour Turnover.'
JRSS Series A, Vol. 122, pp. 232–239, 1959.

32 BARTHOLOMEW, D. J.
'Two-stage Replacement Strategies.'
ORQ, Vol. 14, pp. 77–93, 1963.

33 BARTHOLOMEW, D. J.
'A Multi-stage Renewal Process.'
JRSS Series B, Vol. 25, pp. 150–168, 1963.

34 BARTHOLOMEW, D. J.
'An Approximate Solution to the Integral Equation of Renewal Theory.'
JRSS Series B, Vol. 25, pp. 432–441, 1963.

35 BARTHOLOMEW, D. J.
Stochastic Models for Social Processes.
Wiley, New York and Chichester, 1967

36 BASS, N.
'Differential Effects of Training on Persons of Different Leadership Status.'

Human Relations, Vol. 7, 1966.

37 BAUMGARTEL,   See No. 358.
    H. J. (with
    MANN, F. C.)

38 BAWA, V. S.   'The Assignment of Co-operating
    (and NAIR, K.)   Workers to Service Automatic
                           Machines.'
                           J. Indust. Eng., Vol. 17, No. 9, p. 491,
                           1966.

39 BEACH, E. F.   *Economic Models.*
                           John Wiley and Sons, New York and
                           Chichester, 1957.

40 BEAUMONT, R. A.   *Management, Automation and People.*
    (and HELFGOTT,   Industrial Relations Counsellers,
    R. B.)   New York, 1964.

41 BECKERMAN, W.   'Projections and Productivity
                           Concepts.'
                           *Planning Education for Economic and
                           Social Development.*
                           OECD, Paris, 1964.

42 BECKWITH, R. E.   See No. 307.
    (with KOSSACK,
    C. F.)

43 BEER, S.   'Operational Research Project on
                           Technical Education.'
                           ORQ, Vol. 13, No. 2, p. 179, 1962.

44 BEHRENDS, H.   'Absence and Labour Turnover in a
                           Changing Economic Climate.'
                           Occupational Psychology, Vol. 27, Part 2,
                           1953.

45 BELL, D.   'Pitfalls in Manpower Planning.'
                           Personnel, Vol. 1, No. 12, p. 42, 1968.

46 BELL, D. (and   'Levies, Grants, and Manpower
    COLEMAN, D.)   Training for Industry.'
                           *Technical Education and Industrial
                           Training*, Vol. 10, No. 5, pp. 201-203,
                           1968.

47 BELL, D. (and   'Fixing the Ideal Levy.'
    COLEMAN, D.)   *Personnel*, Vol. 1, No. 3, pp. 24–25,
                           1968.

48 BELL, D. (with   See No. 292.
     JONES, G.,
     COLEMAN, D.,
     and CENTER, A.)

49 BELL, E. J. (with   See No. 455.
     PRESTON, L. E.)

50 BENNIS, W. G.   *Changing Organisations.*
                          McGraw-Hill, New York and
                          Maidenhead, 1966.

51 BENTLEY, F. R.   *People, Productivity, and Progress.*
                          Business Publications, 1964.

52 BEREDAY, G. Z.   *The World Yearbook of Education,* 1967.
     (BLAUG, M. and   *Educational Planning.*
     LAUWERYS, V.)   Evans Bros., London, 1967.

53 BERENSCHOT, B. W.   *Training to Meet Problems of
                          Technological Change.*
                          Australian Institute of Industrial
                          Research, 1963.

54 BERRY, N. H.   *Attitudes of Marines during First
                          Enlistment.*
                          Report No. 21.
                          Naval Medical Neuropsychiatric
                          Research Unit, USA, 1966.

55 BESHERS, J. M.   'Birth Projection with Cohort Models.'
                          Demography, Vol. 2, p. 593, 1965.

56 BHALLA, A. S.   'Manpower Planning in the Context of
                          Perspective Economic Planning in
                          Pakistan.'
                          International Labor Review, Vol. 96,
                          p. 468, 1967.

57 BISHOP, S. V.   *Business Planning and Control.*
                          ICA, London, 1966.

58 BISRA   *Manpower and Investment Expenditure.*
                          Report No. OR/17/68, BISRA, Inter-
                          Group Laboratories of the British
                          Steel Corporation, London, 1968.

59 BISRA   *Forecasting and Planning Training Loads
                          in the Steel Industry.*
                          Report No. OR/47/68 and appendices.
                          BISRA, Inter-Group Laboratories of the
                          British Steel Corporation, London, 1969.

60 BLACK, W.   *Costs and Benefits of Industrial Training.*
                        Northern Ireland Training Council,
                        Queen's, Belfast, to be published.

61 BLAKE, R. (and   *The Managerial Grid.*
    MOUTON, J. S.)   GULF, Houston, Texas, USA, 1964.

62 BLANK, D. M. (and   *The Demand and Supply of Scientific*
    STIGLER, G.)   *Personnel.*
                        National Bureau of Economic
                        Research, New York, 1957.

63 BLAUG, M. (ed.)   *Economics of Education.*
                        Penguin Books, London and
                        Baltimore, Md., 1968.

64 BLAUG, M.   *Utilization of Educated Manpower in*
    (PESTON, M., and   *Industry.*
    ZIEDERMAN, A.)   Oliver and Boyd, London, 1966.

65 BLAUG, M. (with   See No. 52.
    BEREDAY, G. Z.
    and
    LAUWERYS, V.)

66 BLUM, J. L.   'Skill Acquisition and Development.'
                        Lectures and Methodological Essays on
                        Educational Planning.
                        OECD, Paris, 1966.

67 BLUMEN, I.   *The Industrial Mobility of Labour as a*
    (KOGAN, M.,   *Probability Process.*
    and   Cornell Univ. Press, Ithaca, New
    McCARTHY,   York, USA, 1955.
    P. J.)

68 BOMBACH, G.   'Long-term Requirements for Qualified
                        Manpower in Relation to Economic
                        Growth.'
                        Economic aspects in Higher Education,
                        OECD, Paris, 1964.

69 BOMBACH, G.   'Forecasting Requirements for Highly-
                        qualified Manpower as a basis for
                        Educational Policy.'
                        Manpower Forecasting in Educational
                        Planning, OECD, Paris, 1966.

70 BOS, H. (with   See No. 572.
    TINBERGEN, J.)

71 BOUVIER, U.   'Comparaisons de Techniques
                          d'Enquete.'
                          Manpower Research in the Defence Context.
                          EUP, London, and American Elsevier,
                          New York, 1969.

72 BOWEN, W. G.   'Labor Force Participation and
    (and   Unemployment.'
    FINAGAN, T. A.)   *Employment Policy and the Labor Market*
                          (ed. Ross, A.)
                          Univ. of California Press, Berkeley,
                          USA, 1965.

73 BOWIE, R. M.   'Factors Affecting Long-Range
                          Research Planning in the Electronic
                          Industry.'

74 BOWMAN, G. (with)   See No. 9.
    ANDERSON, R. G.)

75 BRANCH, M. C.   *The Corporate Planning Process.*
                          AMA, New York, 1962.

76 BRANCH, M. C.   'A View of Corporate Planning
                          Today.'
                          California Management Review, Winter,
                          1964.

77 BRANDENBURG,   'Anatomy of Corporate Planning.'
    R. G.   *Harvard Business Review,* Nov./Dec.,
                          1962.

78 BRECH, R.   'The Pitfalls of Planning.'
                          Times Review of Business and Technology,
                          Oct., 1965.

79 BRECHLING, F.   'The Relationship between Output
                          and Employment in British Manu-
                          facturing Industry.'
                          Review of Economic Studies, Vol. 32,
                          p. 187, 1865.

80 BRITISH   *Manpower Planning in the British*
    PETROLEUM   *Petroleum Company.*
                          BP, London and Paris, 1967.

81 BROSTER, E. J.   'The Learning Curve for Labour.'
                          Business Management, pp. 34–37,
                          March, 1968.

82 BROWN, A.   *Economic Growth and Manpower.*
    (STONE, R.,   British Association for Commercial and

	PYATT, G., and LEICESTER, C.)	Industrial Education, London, 1963.
83	BROWN, M. (ed.)	*The Theory and Empirical Analysis of Production.* Columbia Univ. Press, New York and London.
84	BROWN W.	*Exploration in Management.* Heinemann, London, 1960. (U.S. distributor, Southern Illinois University Press.
85	BROWN, W.	*Piecework Abandoned.* Heinemann, London, 1962. (U.S. distributor, Southern Illinois University Press.)
86	BROWN, W. (with JAQUES, E.)	See No. 282.
87	BRUNNER, W. G.	'REACT for Precise Manpower Control.' *Financial Executive*, July, 1967.
88	BRYANT, D. T.	'A Survey of the Development of Manpower Planning Policies.' *B. Journ. Ind. Rel.*, Vol. 3, pp. 279–290, 1965.
89	BURGESS, T. (LAYARD, R., AND PANT, P.)	*Manpower and Educational Development in India*, 1961–1986. Oliver and Boyd, London, 1968.
90	BURGOYNE, J.	'Analysing the Induction Crisis.' *Personnel*, Vol. 1, Part 7, pp. 32–35, June, 1968.
91	BURNS, T. (and STALKER, G. M.)	*The Management of Innovation.* Tavistock Publications, London, 1961. (U.S. distributor, Barnes and Noble, New York.)
92	BUZZARD, R. B. (and RADFORTH, J. L.)	*Statistical Records about People at Work.* Report 16, Nat. Inst. Indust. Psych., London, 1964.
93	CAIN, G. C.	'Unemployment and Labor-Force Participation of Secondary Workers.' *Industrial and Labor Relations Review*, Vol. 20, pp. 257–297, Jan., 1967.

94 CAIN, G. C.   'Occupational Classification—An
    (HANSEN, W. L.   Economic Approach.'
    and WEISBROD,   *Monthly Labor Review*, Vol. 90, No. 2,
    B. A.)   pp. 48–52, 1967.

95 CAINE, J. A. J.   'Cost of Training Apprentices in 7
                        Victorian Undertakings.'
                        Personnel Practice Bulletin, Vol. 20, No. 1
                        Dept. of Labour, Australia, 1965.

96 CANNO, W. M.   *Multinational Corporate Planning*.
                        Macmillan, New York, 1966.

97 CARMICHAEL, J. D.   'Long Range Business Planning—
                        Predicting the Unpredictable.'
                        British Industry, March, 1967.

98 CARROLL, D. C.   'Man-machine Co-operation on
                        Planning and Control Problems.'
                        Industrial Management Review, Autumn,
                        1966.

99 CARTER, D.   'Evaluating the Performance of Indi-
                        viduals as Members of Small Groups.'
                        Personnel Psychology, Vol. 7, 1964.

100 CARTER, M.   *Into Work*.
                        Penguin Books, London and Baltimore,
                        Md., 1966.

101 CASSELL, F. H.   'Manpower Planning—the Basic
                        Policies.'
                        Personnel (*AMA*), pp. 55–65, Nov.,
                        1965.

102 CASSIDY, R. E.   'Manpower Planning—a Co-ordinated
                        Approach.'
                        Personnel (*AMA*), pp. 35–45, Sept.,
                        1963.

103 CELLERMAN,   *Motivation and Productivity*.
    S. W.   AMA, New York, 1963.

104 CENTER, A. (with   See No. 292.
    Jones, G.,
    BELL, D., and
    COLEMAN, D.)

105 CHADWICK, E.   'An Approach to Manpower Planning.'
    (and   *Personnel Management*, Vol. 49, pp. 141–
    DUFFETT, R.)   147, 1967.

106	CHAMBERLAIN, N. W.	*The Firm.* McGraw-Hill, New York and Maidenhead, 1962.
107	CHAMBERLAIN, N. W.	*Private and Public Planning.* McGraw-Hill, New York and Maidenhead, 1962.
108	CHANDLER, A. D.	*Chapters in the History of the Industrial Enterprise.* MIT Press, Mass., USA, 1962.
109	CHAPLIN, D.	'The Turn-over Index.' *B. Journ. Ind. Rel.*, Vol. 6, pp. 75–78, 1968.
110	CHARNES, A. (COOPER, W., and NIEHAUS, R.)	*A Goal Programming Model for Manpower Planning.* M.S.R. Report 115, Carnegie Mellon Univ., Pittsburg, USA, 1967.
111	CLAGUE, E.	'Effects of Technological Change on Occupational Employment Patterns in the US.' *Requirements of Automated Jobs.* Supplement, Final Report of North American Joint Conference, 1964, OECD, Paris, 1965.
112	CLAQUE, D.	*Measurement of Technological Change.* Geneva International Institute for Labour Studies, Geneva, 1964.
113	CLARK, D. G.	*The Industrial Manager—His Background and Career Pattern.* Business Publications, London, 1966.
114	CLARK, D. G. (with MOSSON, T. M.)	See No. 391.
115	CLAUSEN, R. (with HARRIS, A. I.)	See No. 230.
116	CLEMENTS, R. V.	*Managers—a Study of their Careers in Industry.* Allen and Unwin, London, 1967.
117	COLEMAN, D. (with BELL, D.)	See No. 46.
118	COLEMAN, D. (with BELL, D.)	See No. 47.

119   COLEMAN, D.   See No. 292.
      (with JONES, G.,
      BELL, D., and
      CENTER, A.)

120   COMBS, W. V.   'Major Manpower Planning Problems.'
                           Manpower Planning, pp. 210–217, EUP,
                           London, and American Elsevier, New
                           York, 1966.

121   CONSTABLE, J. H.   *Group Assessment Programs — The*
                           Measurement of Indirect Work.
                           Business   Publications,   New   York,
                           1966.

122   COOPER, S. (and   'Labor Force Projections for 1970–
      JOHNSTON, D.)   1980.'
                           Monthly Labor Review, Vol. 88, No. 2,
                           pp. 129–140, 1965.

123   COPPER, W. W.   *New Perspectives in Organisation Research.*
      (LEAVITT, H. J.,   John Wiley and Sons, New York and
      and   Chichester, 1966.
      SHELLEY, M.)

124   COOPER, W. W.   See No. 110.
      (with CHARNES,
      A., and
      NIEHAUS, R.)

125   CORREA, H. (with   See No. 571.
      TINBERGEN, J.)

126   COTTERILL, D. S.   'A Model for Personnel Inventory
                           Prediction.'
                           Manpower Research in the Defence Context.
                           EUP, London, and American Elsevier,
                           New York, 1969.

127   COUTIE, G. A.   *Short-Term Forecasting.*
                           Monograph No. 2, ICI Mathematical
                           and Statistical Techniques for
                           Industry.
                           Oliver and Boyd, 1964.

128   COX, D. R. (and   'On the Super-Position of Renewal
      SMITH, W. L.)   Processes.'
                           Biometrika, Vol. 41, pp. 91–99, 1954.

129   COX, D. R.   *Renewal Theory.*
                           Methuen, London, 1962.

130 CREAMER, D. 'Measuring Job Vacancies—
A Feasibility Study in Rochester.'
Proceedings National Industrial
Conference, New York, 1967.

131 CREAMER, D. (with See No. 296.
KENDRICK, J. W.)

132 CRONBACH, L. J. *Psychological Tests and Personnel*
(and GLESER, *Decisions.*
E. C.) Illinois Univ. Press, USA, 1957.

133 CROSBY. A. *Creativity and Performance in Industrial*
Organisations.
Tavistock Publications, London, 1968.
(U.S. distributor, Barnes and Noble,
New York.)

134 CROSSLEY, J. R. 'Essential Statistics for Manpower
Forecasting.'
Manpower Policy and Employment Trends.
G. Bell and Sons, London, 1966.

135 CROSSLEY, J. R. 'Forecasting Manpower Demand and
Supply.'
Manpower Policy and Employment Trends.
G. Bell and Sons, London, 1966.

136 CROSSMAN, E. F. 'A Model for the Prediction of Manpower Requirements.'
Monthly Labor Review, Vol. 88, No. 6,
pp. 669–671, June, 1965.

137 CURRIE, R. M. *Work Study.*
BIM, London, 1965.

138 DALE, E. *Long Range Planning.*
BIM, London, 1967.

139 DARMSTADTER, J. 'Manpower in a Long-term Economic
Projection Model.'
Industrial Relations, May, 1966.

140 DERNBERG, T. 'Hidden Unemployment 1953–1962;
(and STRAND, a Quantitative Analysis by Age and
K.) Sex.'
American Economic Review, Vol. 56,
p. 71, 1966.

141 DERNBERG, T. 'A Parametric Approach to Labor
(STRAND, K., Force Projection.'

and Dukler, J.)   *Industrial Relations*, Vol. 6, No. 1, pp. 46–68, 1966.

142   DEVINNEY, L. C.   *The American Soldier—Adjustment during Army Life.*
Princetown Univ. Press, USA, 1949.

143   DE WITT, N.   *Education and Professional Employment in the USSR.*
National Science Foundation, Washington, DC, 1961.

144   DILL, W. R. (and GAVER, A.)   'Models and Modelling for Manpower Planning.'
J. Man. Science, Vol. 13B, p. 142, 1964.

145   DOOS, STEN-OLOF   'Forecasting Manpower Requirements by Occupational Categories.'
Planning Education for Economic and Social Development (ed. PARNES, H. S.)
OECD, Paris, 1963.

146   DORFMAN, R.   *Econometric Analysis for Assessing the Efficacy of Public Investment.*
Pontifical Academy of Science, Vatican City, 1964.

147   DORN, H. F.   'Pitfalls in Population Forecasts and Projections.'
JASA, Vol. 45, pp. 311–334, 1950.

148   DOTY, J. H.   'Human Capital Budgeting—Maximising Returns in Training Investment.'
J. Ind. Eng., Vol. 16, No. 2, 1965.

149   DOWNS, S.   'Labour Turnover in Two Public Service Organisations.'
Occupational Psychology, Vol. 41, pp. 137–142, 1967.

150   DRENTH, P. J. D.   'Some Current Issues in Selection and Placement Research.'
Manpower Planning, pp. 3–26, EUP, London, 1966.

151   DRUI, A. B.   'The Use of Regression Equations to Predict Manpower Requirements.'
Management Science, Vol. 9, July, 1963.

152   DUBOIS, P. H.   'Aspects of the Criterion Problem in Personnel Research.'

Manpower Planning, EUP, London, and American Elsevier, New York, 1966.

153 DUFFETT, R. (with CHADWICK, E. S.) See No. 105.

154 DUIJKER, H. C. (and FRIJEDA, N. H.) *National Character and National Stereotypes.* North Holland Publishing Co., Amsterdam, 1960.

155 DUKLER, J. (with DERNBERG, T., and STRAND, K.) See No. 141.

156 DUNCAN, K. (with ANNETTE, J.) See No. 11.

157 DUNLOP, J. T. (and DIATCHENKO, V.) (eds.) *Labor Productivity.* McGraw-Hill, New York and Maidenhead, 1964.

158 DUNNETTE, M. D. *Personnel Selection and Placement.* Tavistock Publications, London, and Wadsworth Publishing Company, California, 1967.

159 DURBIN, J. *Manpower Allocation and Mathematical Programming.* Research Publication 3553. Rand Corporation of America, Santa Monica, Cal., USA, 1964.

160 DURBIN, J. (and WRIGHT, R.) *Model for Estimating Military Personnel Requirement.* Research Publication 5398, Rand Corporation of America, Santa Monica, Cal., USA, 1966.

161 DURHAM, W. A. *Personnel Records, Forms and Procedures.* Industry Society, 1965.

162 DURMAN, L. *Selection, Training, and Management of Staff.* ICA, London, 1966.

163 EASTERFIELD, T. E. *Productivity Measurement in Great Britain.* DSIR, London, 1959.

164 ECKSTEIN, O. (and WILSON, T.) 'Short-run Productivity Behavior in US Manufacturing.' *Review of Economics and Statistics*, Vol. 46, pp. 41–54, 1964.

165 EIRE NATIONAL   *Report on Manpower.*
     INDUSTRIAL   Stationery Office, Dublin, Eire, 1964.
     ECONOMIC
     COUNCIL

166 ELECTRICITE DE   'Les Progrès de Productivité et leur
     FRANCE   Utilization à l'Electricité de France,
                        1952 à 1962.'
                        Etudes et Conjoncture, No. 1, 1965.

167 EMMERIJ, L. J.   'Projecting Manpower Requirements
     (and THIAS, H.)   by Occupation.'
                        *Lectures and Methodological Essays on
                        Educational Planning,*
                        OECD, Paris, 1966.

168 ENKE, P.   'Economic Effects of Slowing Popula-
                        tion Growth.'
                        Economic Journal, Vol. 76, p. 1, 1966.

169 EUROPEAN COAL   *Methods used in E.C.S.C. Surveys on the
     and STEEL   Social Consequences of Technological
     COMMUNITY   Change.*
                        ILO, Geneva, 1964.

170 EUROPEAN   *Steel Workers and Technical Progress—
     PRODUCTIVITY   a Comparative Report on Six National
     AGENCY   Studies.*
                        European Productivity Agency,
                        Paris, 1959.

171 EWING, D. W. (ed.) *Long Range Planning for Management.*
                        Harper and Row, New York, 1963.

172 EWING, D. W.   'Corporate Planning at the Cross-
                        roads.'
                        Harvard Business Review, July/Aug.,
                        1967.

173 FARRAG, A. M.   'The Value of Occupational-Industry
                        Data for Forecasting Purposes.'
                        International Labor Review, April, 1967.

174 FARRIMOND, H. L.   *Determining Present and Future Require-
                        ments.*
                        UK Ministry of Labour, 1966.

175 FERBER, R.   *Employers' Forecasts of Manpower
                        Requirements.*
                        Bureau of Economic and Business
                        Research, Univ. of Illinois, USA, 1958.

176 FERRARO, E. T. 'The Role of Manpower Research in military manpower management.'
Manpower Research in the Defence Context.
EUP, London, and American Elsevier, New York, 1969.

177 FERREL, R. W. *Customer-Oriented Planning.*
AMA, New York, USA, 1964.

178 FINK, F. *Projected Manpower Needs.*
Research Publication 15,
George Washington University, USA, 1966.

179 FISHER, F. M. 'Re-enlistments in the US Navy—a Cost-effectiveness Study.'
American Economic Review, Vol. 57, No. 2, 1967.

180 FISHER, F. M. 'Aspects of Cost-Benefit Analysis in Defence Manpower Planning.'
Manpower Research in the Defence Context.
EUP, London, and American Elsevier, New York, 1969.

181 FIX, E. (and NEYMAN, J.) 'A Simple Stochastic Model of Recovery, Relapse, Death, and Loss of Patients.'
Human Biology, Vol. 23, pp. 205-241, 1951.

182 FLANDERS, A. *The Fawley Productivity Agreements.*
Faber and Faber, London, 1964.

183 FOGARTHY, M. P. 'Wage and Salary Policies for Recruitment.'
B. Journ. Ind. Rel., Vol. 3, No. 3, p. 311, 1965.

184 FOLEY, M. A. 'Operations Research in Aer Lingus.'
JRAeS, Vol. 72, pp. 596–602, 1968.

185 FOLGER, J. K. (and NAM, C. B.) 'Trends in Education in Relation to Occupational Structure.'
Sociology of Education, Autumn, 1967.

186 FORRESTER, J. W. *Industrial Dynamics.*
Wiley, New York and Chichester, 1961.

187 FOX, A. *Time Span of Discretion Theory—an Appraisal.*
IPM, London, 1966.

188 FRANCIS, J. P.   'Technological Change, Productivity, and Employment in Canada.'
Requirements of Automated Jobs.
Supplement, Final Report of the North American Joint Conference, 1964.
OECD, Paris, 1965.

189 FRIJEDA, N. H.   See No. 154.
(with DUIJKER, H. C.)

190 FULMER, J. L.   *Research Design to Forecast Demand for*
(GREEN, R. E.   *new types of technicians in an industry.*
and HAIN, P. B.)   Office of Technical Services—A.D603110.
Washington DC, USA, 1966.

191 GADET, M. S.   See No. 311.
(with KRIEDT, P. H.)

192 GALES, K. (and   *Manpower Demand Forecasts for the Social*
WRIGHT, R. C.)   *Services.*
National Council for Social Service, London, 1966.

193 GANI, J.   'Formulae for Projecting Enrolments and Degrees Awarded in Universities.'
JRSS Series A, Vol. 126, pp. 400–409, 1963.

194 GASCOIGNE, I. M.   'Manpower Forecasting at the Enterprise Level.'
B. Journ. Ind. Rel., Vol. 6, Part 1, pp. 94–106, 1968.

195 GAUDET, F. J.   *Labour Turnover—Calculation and Cost.*
Research Study 39, AMA, New York, 1960.

196 GAUDET, F. J.   *Solving the Problems of Employee Absence.*
Research Study 57, AMA, New York, 1967.

197 GAVER, A. (with   See No. 144.
DILL, W. R.)

198 GEISLER, E. B.   *Manpower Planning—an Emerging Staff Function.*
Bulletin 101, AMA, New York, 1967.

199	GHISELLI, E. E.	*The Validity of Occupational Aptitude Tests.* Wiley, New York and Chichester, 1966.
200	GILMORE, F. F.	'Anatomy of Corporate Planning.' *Harvard Business Review*, Nov./Dec., 1962.
201	GILMORE, F. F.	'Strategic Planning's Threat to Small Businesses.' *California Management Review*, Dec., 1966.
202	GINSBERG, E.	*Manpower Strategy in Developing Countries.* Wiley, New York and Chichester, 1967.
203	GLASS, D. V. (ed.)	*Social Mobility in Britain.* Routledge and Kegan Paul, London, 1954.
204	GLESER, E. C. (with CRONBACH, L. J.)	See No. 132.
205	GOLDSTEIN, H.	'An Evaluation of Experience in Long-term Projections of Employment by Education.' *21st Interstate Conference on Labor Statistics*, California, June, 1963.
206	GOLDSTEIN, H.	'Projections of Manpower Requirements and Supply.' *Industrial Relations*, May, 1966.
207	GOLDSTEIN, H. (and SWERDLOFF, S.)	*Methods of Long-Term Projection of Requirements for, and Supply of, Qualified Manpower.* UNESCO, Paris, 1967.
208	GORDON, L. V.	*Manual for Survey of Interpersonal Values.* Science Research Associates, Chicago, 1960.
209	GORDON, R. A. (ed.)	*Long-Term Manpower Projections.* Institute of Industrial Relations, Univ. of California, Berkeley, 1965.
210	GORHAM, W.	*Some Analytical Techniques for Personnel Planning.* Rand Corporation of America, Santa Monica, Cal., USA, 1960.

211 GORHAM, W.   'An Application of a Network Flow
                         Model to Personnel Planning.'
                         IEEE, Vol. EM–10, No. 3, pp. 121–
                         123, 1963.

212 GORHAM, W.   'US Draft Study.'
                         Manpower Planning, pp. 157–183,
                         EUP, London, and American Elsevier,
                         New York, 1966.

213 GOWLER, D.   'Determinants of the Supply of Labour
                         to the Firm.'
                         J. Man. Stud., Vol. 6, No. 1, pp. 73-95,
                         1969.

214 GRAIS, B.   *Forecasting of the Active Population by
                         Occupation and Level of Skill.*
                         OECD, Paris, 1966.

215 GRAY, D. H.   *Manpower Planning.*
                         IPM, London, 1966.

216 GREEN, R. E.   See No. 190.
     (with FULMER,
     J. L., and
     HAIN, P. B.)

217 GREENBERG, L.   'Technological Change, Productivity,
                         and Employment in the United States.'
                         Requirements of Automated Jobs.
                         Supplement, Final Report of the
                         North American Joint Conference,
                         1964.
                         OECD, Paris, 1965.

218 GREENBERGER, M.   See No. 426.
     (with ORCUTT,
     G. H., KORBEL,
     J., and
     RIVLIN, E.)

219 GREENFIELD,   *Manpower and the Growth of the Product
     H. I.   Services.*
                         Columbia Univ. Press, New York, 1966.

220 GREGG, J. V.   *Mathematical Trends Curves—an Aid to
                         Forecasting.*
                         ICI Mathematical and Statistical
                         Techniques for Industry, Monograph
                         No. 1, Oliver and Boyd, London, 1964.

221 GROSS, E. 'When Occupations Meet—Professions in Trouble.'
Industrial Relations Centre,
University of Minnesota,
Minneapolis, USA, 1967.

222 HAASE, P. E. 'Technological Change and Manpower Forecasts.'
Industrial Relations, Vol. 5, No. 3, pp. 59–71, 1966.

223 HAIN, P. B. (with GREEN, R. E. and FULMER, J. L.) See No. 190.

224 HALFORD, D. R. C. *Business Planning.*
Pan, London, 1968.

225 HALL, M. 'Towards a Manpower Grid.'
Personnel Management, Vol. 47, pp. 72–78, 1965.

226 HARBISON, F. H. (and MYERS, C. A.) *Education, Manpower, and Economic Growth.*
McGraw-Hill, New York and Maidenhead, 1964.

227 HARBISON, F. H. (and MYERS, C. A.) *Manpower and Education.*
McGraw-Hill, New York and Maidenhead, 1965.

228 HARDING, F. D. (and MEREK, J.) *Markov Chain Theory Applied to the Prediction of Retirement Rates.*
Personnel Research Lab., Lackland Air Force Base, USA, 1964.

229 HARPER, S. F. (with WHISTLER, T. L.) See No. 681.

230 HARRIS, A. I. (and CLAUSEN, R.) *Labour Mobility in Great Britain, 1953–1963.*
HMSO, London, 1966.

231 HARRIS, M. (ed.) *The Realities of Productivity Bargaining.*
IPM, London, 1968.

232 HART, P. E. (and PRAIS, S.) 'The Analysis of Business Concentration.'
JRSS Series A, Vol. 119, pp. 150–191, 1956.

233 HEDBERG, M.   'Turnover of Labour in Industry—an
                              Actuarial Study.'
                              Acta Sociologica, Vol. 5, pp. 129–143,
                              1961.

234 HELFGOTT, R. B.   See No. 40.
     (with
     BEAUMONT, R. A.)

235 HERBST, P. G.   'Organisational Commitment—
                              a Decision Process Model.'
                              Acta Sociologica, Vol. 7, pp. 34–45, 1963.

236 HERMANSON, R. H.   *Accounting for Human Assets.*
                              Bureau of Business and Economic
                              Research, Michigan State University,
                              USA, 1964.

237 HERRENSTART,   See No. 251.
     I. L. (with
     HOROWITZ, M.,
     and
     ZYMELMAN, M.)

238 HERZBERG, F.   *The Motivation to Work.*
                              Wiley, New York and Chichester, 1959.

239 HICKEY, J. T.   'Guidelines in Successful Future
                              Planning.'
                              Financial Executive, Nov., 1966.

240 HILAND, R. E. (and   *Work Sampling.*
     RICHARDSON,   McGraw-Hill, New York and
     W. J.)   Maidenhead, USA, 1957.

241 HILL, J. M.   'A Consideration of Labour Turnover
                              as the Result of a Quasi-stationery
                              Process.'
                              Human Relations, Vol. 4, pp. 255-264,
                              1951.

242 HILL, J. M.   'A Note on Time-span and Economic
                              Theory.'
                              Human Relations, Vol. 11, No. 4, 1958.

243 HILL, J. M.   *A Study of Labour Turnover in the Food
                              Processing Industry.*
                              Tavistock Publications, London, 1967.

244 HILL, J. M. (with   See No. 470.
     RICE, A. K., and
     TRIST, E.)

245 HINRICHES, J. R.   *High Talent Personnel.*
                          AMA, New York, USA, 1966.

246 HITCH, C. J.   *The Economics of Defence in the Nuclear Age.*
                          Harvard University Press, USA, 1960.

247 HODGSON, P. R.   'Manpower Planning—at the Level of the Firm.'
                          BACIE Journal, pp. 150–157, 1965.

248 HOLLISTER, R. G.   'The Economics of Manpower Forecasting.'
                          International Labour Review, April, 1964.

249 HOLLISTER, R. G.   *Technical Evaluation of the Mediterranean Regional Project.*
                          OECD, Paris, 1966.

250 HOOD, R. C.   'Concern for Cost—a Participative Approach.'
                          AMA, New York, USA, 1956.

251 HOROWITZ, M. A.   *Manpower Requirements for Planning—an*
     (ZYMELMAN, M.   *International Comparison Approach.*
     and   Vols. 1 and 2.
     HERRENSTADT,   North-eastern University, Boston,
     I. L.)   Mass., USA, 1966.

252 HUFNER, K.   'Economics of Higher Education and Educational Planning—a Bibliography.'
                          Socio-Economic Planning Sciences,
                          Vol. 2, pp. 25–101, 1968.

253 HULTGREN, T.   *Changes in Labor Cost during Cycles in Production and Business.*
                          Occasional Paper 74.
                          National Bureau of Economic Research, New York, USA, 1960.

254 HUMBLE, J.   *Improving Management Performance.*
                          BIM, London, 1965.

255 HUMBLE, T. N.   *Standards in Strategic Planning and Control.*
                          Bureau of Business Research, University of Texas, USA, 1966.

256 HUSSEY, D.   'Why and How of Strategic Planning.'
                          Business, Jan., 1967.

257 HUTCHINGS, D.   *The Science Undergraduate.*
                          Dept. of Education,
                          University of Oxford, UK, 1968.
258 ICWA   *An Introduction to Business Forecasting.*
                          Institute of Costs and Works
                          Accountants, London, 1959.
259 ILO   *Measurement of Under-Employment.*
                          ILO, Geneva, 1957.
260 ILO   *A Tabulation of Case Studies on
                          Technological Change.*
                          ILO, Geneva, 1963.
261 ILO   *Automation—Research Methods.*
                          ILO, Geneva, 1964.
262 ILO   *Social Effects of Automation—Abstracts.*
                          ILO, Geneva, 1964.
263 ILO   *International Differences in Factors
                          Affecting Labour Mobility.*
                          ILO, Geneva, 1965.
264 ILO   *Technological Changes and Manpower in a
                          Centrally Planned Economy.*
                          ILO, Geneva, 1966.
265 ILO   *Management and Adjustment Programs.*
                          ILO, Geneva, 1967.
266 ILO   *Automation and Non-manual Workers.*
                          ILO, Geneva, 1967.
267 INDIK, B. P.   See No. 359.
     (with MANN,
     F. C., and
     VROOM, V. H.)
268 INDUSTRIAL   *The Effective Use of People.*
     SOCIETY   Industrial Society, London, 1967.
269 INKELES, A. (and   *Handbook of Social Psychology.*
     LEVINSON, D. J.)   Addison-Wesley, Cambridge, Mass.,
                          USA, 1954.
270 INTERNATIONAL   *Symposium on Forecasting of Manpower
     MANPOWER   Requirements.*
     INSTITUTE   Washington DC, USA, 1966.
271 IRISH   *Planning Your Business.*
     MANAGEMENT   National Industrial Economic Council,
     INSTITUTE   Dublin Stationery Office, Eire, 1966.

E

272 ISAAC, J. E.   'Manpower Planning in Australia.'
International Labour Review, Nov., 1960.

273 JACOBS, E. E. (with   See No. 314.
KUTSCHER, R. E.)

274 JAKUBAUSKAS,   'Technological Change and Recent
E. B.   Trends in the Composition of Railroad
Employment.'
Quarterly Review of Economics and Business, Nov., 1962.

275 JANTSCH, E.   *Technological Forecasting in Perspective.*
OECD, Paris, 1967.

276 JAQUES, E.   'The Social and Psychological Impact of a Change in Method of Wage Payment.'
Human Relations, Vol. 4, No. 4, 1951.

277 JAQUES, E.   *Measurement of Responsibility.*
Tavistock Publications, London, 1956.
(U.S. distributor, Barnes and Noble, New York.)

278 JAQUES, E.   'Standard Earning Progression Curves.'
Human Relations, Vol. 11, No. 2, 1958.

279 JAQUES, E.   'Objective Measures for Pay Differentials.'
Harvard Business Review, Jan./Feb., 1962.

280 JAQUES, E.   *Time-Span Handbook.*
Heinemann, London, 1964.
(U.S. distributor, Southern Illinois University Press.)

281 JAQUES, E.   *Progression Handbook.*
Heinemann, London, and Southern Illinois University Press, 1964.

282 JAQUES, E. (and   *Glacier Project Papers.*
BROWN, W.)   Heinemann, London, 1965.
(U.S. distributor, Southern Illinois University Press.)

283 JAQUES, E.   *Equitable Payment.*
Penguin Books, London and Baltimore, Md., 1967.

284 JESSOP, W. N. (ed.)   *Manpower Planning.*

		EUP, London, and American Elsevier New York, 1966.
285	JOHNSTON, D. F.	*Long Range Projections of Labor Force.* Bureau of Labor Statistics. Dept. of Labor, USA, 1967.
286	JOHNSTON, T. L.	*State Policy—Company Practice.* Personnel, Vol. 1, No. 2, Jan., 1968.
287	JONES, E.	'An Actuarial Problem Concerning the Royal Marines.' *JIA Stud. Soc.*, Vol. 6, pp. 38–42, 1946.
288	JONES, E.	'The Application of the Sevice-Table Technique to Staffing Problems.' *JIA Stud. Soc.*, Vol. 8, pp. 49–55, 1948.
289	JONES, E.	'The Application of Actuarial Techniques to Officer Career Planning.' *Manpower Research in the Defence Context.* EUP, London, and American Elsevier, New York, 1969.
290	JONES, E. O. (and MORRELL, S. G.)	'Environmental Forecasting in British Industry.' *J. Man. Stud.*, Feb., 1966.
291	JONES, G.	'The Needs of Industry.' *Journal CRAC*, Vol. 1, Part 2, 1964.
292	JONES, G. (BELL, D., COLEMAN, D. and CENTER, A.)	*Perspectives in Manpower Planning, an Edinburgh Group Report.* IPM, London, 1967.
293	JORGENSEN, D. W. (and GRILICHES, Z.)	'The Explanation of Productivity Change.' *Review of Economic Studies*, Vol. 34, pp. 249–283, 1967.
294	KENDALL, M. G.	*Statistics and Personnel Management.* IPM, London, 1965.
295	KENDALL, M. G.	'Mathematical Models in Manpower Planning.' *Manpower Research in the Defence Context.* EUP, London, and American Elsevier, New York, 1969.
296	KENDRICK, J. W. (and CREAMER, J.)	*Measuring Company Productivity.* US National Industrial Conference Board, 1964.

297	KERR, W. A.	'Labour Turnover and its Correlates.' *J. App. Psych.*, Vol. 31, pp. 366–371, 1947.
298	KILBRIDGE, C.	'Economic Models for the Division of Labour.' *Management Science*, Vol. 12, pp. 8–25, 1966.
299	KIVIAT, P. J.	*Manpower Requirements Prediction and Allocation for Aircraft Maintenance.* Research Publication 5215, Rand Corp. of America, USA, 1966.
300	KLECKA, J.	'An Application of Linear Programming for the Determination of the Minimum Cost Labor Mixture under the Conditions of Varying Production Levels.' *Proc. Amer. Inst. Ind. Eng.*, New York, USA, 1962.
301	KLUBECK, N.	'Differential Effects of Training on Persons of Different Leadership Status.' *Human Relations*, Vol. 7, 1964.
302	KNIGHT, R.	'Changes in the Occupational Structure of the Working Population.' *JRSS Series A*, Vol. 130, p. 3, 1967.
303	KNOWLES, M. C.	'A Review of Labour Turnover Research.' *Personnel Practice Bulletin*, pp. 25–37, March, 1964.
304	KOGAN, M. (with BLUMEN, I., and McCARTHY, P. J.)	See No. 67.
305	KORBEL, A.	'Labor Force Entry and Attachment of Young People.' *JASA*, Vol. 10, 1961.
306	KORBEL, A. (with ORCUTT, G. H., GREENBERGER, M., and RIVLIN, E.)	See No. 426.

307 KOSSACK, C. F.   *The Mathematics of Personnel Utilization*
     (and   *Models.*
     BECKWITH, R.)   Purdue Univ., Lafayette, Ind., USA,
                           1959.

308 KOSSACK, C. F.   'Manpower Systems and Operations
                           Research.'
                           Manpower Planning, pp. 231–256.
                           EUP, London, and American Elsevier,
                           New York, 1966.

309 KOSSACK, C. F.   'A Systems Analyst Approach to the
                           Theory of Manpower Management.'
                           Manpower Research in the Defence Context.
                           EUP, London, and American Elsevier,
                           New York, 1969.

310 KRAUCH, H.   'Resistance against Analysis and
                           Planning in Research and
                           Development.'
                           Management Science, Vol. 13, 1967.

311 KREIDT, P. H. (and   'Prediction of Labour Turnover among
     GADEL, M. S.)   Clerical Workers.'
                           J. App. Psych., Vol. 37, p. 338, 1965.

312 KUH, E.   'Cyclical and Secular Labor
                           Productivity in US Manufacturing.'
                           Review of Economics and Statistics, Vol. 47.

313 KUHN, J. W.   *Scientific and Managerial Manpower in
                           the Nuclear Industry.*
                           Columbia Univ. Press, New York,
                           1966.

314 KUTSCHER, R. E.   'Factors Affecting Changes in
     (and   Industrial Employment.'
     JACOBS, E. E.)   *Monthly Labor Review*, pp. 7–12, April,
                           1967.

315 LADINSKY, J.   'Sources of Geographic Mobility
                           among Professional Workers: a
                           Multivariate Analysis.'
                           Demography, Vol. 4, No. 1, pp. 293–
                           309, 1967.

316 LANDER, K. E.   'Long-term Growth and Profit.'
                           International Management, Oct., 1966.

317 LANE, K. F. (and   'A Method of Labour Turnover
     ANDREW, J. E.)   Analysis.'

		JRSS Series A, Vol. 118, pp. 296-323, 1955.
318	LANG, G. (with BARRETT, L.)	See No. 30.
319	LAUWERYS, V. A. (with BEREDAY, G. Z., and BLAUG, M.)	See No. 52.
320	LAVE, L. B.	*Technological Change: Its Conception and Measurement.* Prentice-Hall, Englewood Cliffs, New Jersey, 1966.
321	LAWRENCE, J. R. (ed.)	*Operational Research and the Social Sciences.* Tavistock Publications, London, 1966. (U.S. distributor, Barnes and Noble, New York.)
322	LAYARD, P. R. G.	'Educational and Occupational Characteristics of Manpower—an International Comparison.' *B. Journ. Ind. Rel.*, Vol. 4, No. 2, pp. 222–266, 1966.
323	LAYARD, P. R. G. (with MOSER, C.)	See No. 390.
324	LEAVITT, H. J. (with COOPER, W. W., and SHELLEY, M.)	See No. 123.
325	LEE, A. M.	'Manpower Planning in an Airline Reservation Office.' *J. Can. Or. Soc.*, Vol. 3, No. 1, pp. 1-11, 1965.
326	LEE, A. M.	*Applied Queuing Theory.* Macmillan, London, 1967. (U.S. distributor, St. Martin's Press, New York.)
327	LEESE, E. L.	'A Dynamic Programming Model as an Aid to the Scheduling of Training.' *Manpower Research in the Defence Context.* EUP, London, and American Elsevier, New York, 1969.

328 LEICESTER, C.   'Economic Growth and the School
                         Leaver.'
                         CRAC Journal, Vol. 1, No. 1, pp. 9–14,
                         1964.

329 LEICESTER, C.   'Methods for Projecting Manpower
                         Coefficients.'
                         OECD, Paris, 1967, mimeographed
                         DAS/EID/67.89)

330 LEICESTER, C.   'The Composition of Manpower
                         Requirements.'
                         Economic Growth and Manpower.
                         BACIE, London, 1963.

331 LEICESTER, C.   'The Manpower Link between
                         Economic Growth and Education—
                         an Analysis of 10 OECD Countries.'
                         OECD, Paris, 1966, mimeographed
                         (DAS/EID/66.5)

332 LEICESTER, C. (ed.) 'Careers of the Future.'
                         Supplement 17 to *Where?* Dec., 1968.

333 LEICESTER, C.   'Manpower Planning for the National
                         Economy—Problems, Concepts, and
                         Methods.'
                         Manpower Research in the Defence Context.
                         EUP, London, and American Elsevier,
                         New York, 1969.

334 LEICESTER, C.   'The National Environment for
                         Manpower Planning.'
                         Cambridge, 1968, to be published.

335 LESIEUR, F. G.   *The Scanlon Plan.*
                         Wiley, New York and Chichester,
                         1959.

336 LESTER, R. A.   *Manpower Planning in a Free Society.*
                         Princeton University Press, USA, 1966.

337 LEVINSON, D. J.   See No. 268.
    (with
    INKELES, A.)

338 LIFF, S. H.   'Computerized Data for Manpower
                         Control.'
                         IEEE, Vol. EM 10, No. 4, pp. 159–
                         165, 1963.

339 LIKERT, R.   *Development Patterns of Management.*

General Management Series No. 178,
pp. 32–51.
AMA, New York, 1955.

340   LIKERT, R.   'Motivational Approach to
Management Development.'
Harvard Business Review, Vol. 37, No. 4.

341   LIKERT, R.   *New Patterns of Management.*
McGraw-Hill, New York and
Maidenhead, 1961.

342   LIKERT, R.   *Human Organization.*
McGraw-Hill, New York and
Maidenhead, 1967.

343   LIKERT, R. (and   'Making Cost Control Work.'
SEASHORE, S. E.)   *Harvard Business Review*, Vol. 41, No. 6,
p. 96, 1963.

344   LINDER, R. W.   See No. 325.
(with LEE, A. M.)

345   LITTELL, A. S.   'Estimation of the T-year Survival
Rate from Follow-up Studies over a
Limited Period of Time.'
Human Biology, Vol. 24, pp. 87-116,
1952.

346   LIVINGSTONE,   'The Use of Regression Equations to
L. L. (and   Predict Manpower Requirements —
MONTGOMERIE,   Critical Comments.'
D.)   *J. Man. Science*, Vol. 12, No. 7, p. 616,
1966.

347   LOASBY, B. J.   'Long-Range Formal Planning in
Perspective.'
J. Man. Stud., Oct., 1967.

348   LOCKYER, K. G.   *An Introduction to Critical Path Analysis.*
Pitman, London and New York, 1964.

349   LUPTON, T.   *Problems of Progress in Industry.*
DSIR, HMSO, London, 1961.

350   LUPTON, T.   *Management and the Social Sciences.*
Hutchinson, London, 1966.

351   LYNCH, E. A.   'Management Information Systems in
Support of Manpower Planning.'
Manpower Planning, pp. 218–228,
EUP, London, and American Elsevier,
New York, 1966.

352 LYNCH, J. J. *Making Manpower Effective—Part 1.*
Pan, London, 1968.

353 LYNN, F. 'An Investigation of the Rate of Development and Diffusion of Technology
in our Modern Society.'
Technology and the American Economy,
Washington, 1966.

354 MADDICK, H. *Use of Costing to Determine Effective and
Economic Use of Available Resources.*
Research Project, Institute of Local
Government, Birmingham University,
UK. To be published.

355 MAIZELS, JOAN 'Changes in Employment Among
School-Leavers.'
B. Journ. Ind. Rel., Vol. 5, No. 2, pp.
211-221, 1967.

356 MALINVAUD, E. *Statistical Methods of Econometrics.*
North Holland Publishing Co.,
Amsterdam, 1966.

357 MANGUM, G. L. 'The Nature and Functions of Man-
(and power Projections.'
NEMORE, A. L.) *Industrial Relations,* Vol. 5, No. 3, p. 1,
1966.

358 MANN, F. C. *The Supervisor's Concern with Costs in an
(and Electric Power Company.*
BAUMGARTEL, Institute for Social Research, Ann
M. J.) Arbor, Mich., 1953.

359 MANN, F. C. *The Productivity of Work Groups.*
(VROOM, V. and Institute for Social Research,
INDIK, G. P.) Ann Arbor, Mich., 1963.

360 MANSFIELD, E. 'Technological Change and the Rate
of Innovation.'
Econometrika, Vol. 29, No. 4, 1961.

361 MANSFIELD, E. 'Technological Change, Measurement
and Diffusion.'
Technology and the American Economy.
Washington, 1966.

362 MANTHEY, P. J. 'Profit Planning using Forecast
Schedules.'
Management Accounting, Jan., 1967.

363 MAPES, R. 'Promotion in Static Hierarchies.'

		J. Man. Stud., Vol. 5, Part 3, pp. 380-387, Oct., 1968.
364	MARCH, J. G. (and SIMON, H. A.)	*Organisations.* Wiley, New York and Chichester, 1958.
365	MARRIOTT, R.	*Incentive Payment Systems.* Staples Press, London, 1957.
366	MARTIN, W. S.	'Long-Range Planning for a Consumer Industry.' *Research Management*, July, 1966.
367	MATRAS, J.	'An Application of the Formal Theory of Social Mobility.' *Population Studies*, Vol. 14, pp. 163-169, 1960.
368	MATRAS, J.	'Differential Fertility . . . and Change in the Occupational Distribution.' *Population Studies*, Vol. 15, pp. 187-197, 1960.
369	MATRAS, J.	'Social Mobility and Social Structure.' *Proceedings of the Sixth World Congress of Sociologists.* Evian, France, 1966.
370	MAYO, E.	*The Human Problems of an Industrial Civilization.* Macmillan, New York, USA, 1933.
371	MAYO, E.	*The Social Problems of an Industrial Civilization.* Routledge and Kegan Paul, London, 1948.
372	McBEATH, G.	*Organisation and Manpower Planning.* Business Publications, London, 1966.
373	McCARTHY, P. J. (with BLUMEN, I, and KOGAN, M.)	See No. 67.
374	McCLELLAND, G.	'Executive Development Within Manpower Plan.' *Business*, pp. 50-57, July, 1966.
375	McCORMICK, E. J. (with TIFFIN, J.)	See No. 569.
376	McGREGOR, D.	*The Human Side of Enterprise.*

McGraw-Hill, New York and
Maidenhead, 1960.

377 McGREGOR, D.   *Leadership and Motivation.*
                        MIT Press, Cambridge, Mass., USA,
                        1966.

378 McGREGOR, D.   'An Uneasy Look at Performance
                        Appraisal.'
                        Harvard Business Review, May/June,
                        1965.

379 MEHMET, O.   *Methods of Forecasting Manpower
                        Requirements.*
                        Department of Labour, Ontario,
                        Canada, 1965.

380 MELTZ, N. M.   *Changes in the Occupational Composition
                        of the Canadian Labour Force, 1931–1961.*
                        Department of Labour, Ottawa, 1965.

381 MEREK, J. (with   See No. 228.
    HARDING, F. D.)

382 MILES, R. E.   'The Affluent Organisation.'
                        Harvard Business Review, Vol. 44, Part 3,
                        pp. 106-114, 1966.

383 MINOR, F. J.   'The Prediction of Turnover of Clerical
                        Employees.'
                        Personnel Psychology, Vol. II, pp. 393–
                        402, 1958.

384 MISRA, R.   'Use of the Time-Span Instruments in
                        Job Analysis and Measurement of
                        Responsibility.'
                        Journ. Inst. Engineers (India), Vol. 42,
                        No. 8, Part GE2.

385 MONK, D.   'The Social Survey in Manpower
                        Research.'
                        Manpower Research in the Defence Context.
                        EUP, London, and American Elsevier,
                        New York, 1964.

386 MONTGOMERIE, D.   See No. 346.
    (with
    LIVINSTONE, J. L.)

387 MORRELL, S. G.   See No. 290.
    (with JONES,
    E. O.)

388   MORTON, A. S.   'Re-Enlistments in the U.S. Navy—
                             A Cost Effectiveness Study.'
                             American Economic Review, Vol. 57,
                             No. 2, 1965.

389   MORTON, A. S.   'Manpower Studies at the Institute of
                             Naval Studies, 1963-66.'
                             Manpower Research in the Defence Context.
                             EUP, London, and American Elsevier,
                             New York, 1969.

390   MOSER, C. A.   'Planning the Scale of Higher Educa-
      (and LAYARD,   tion in Great Britain—Some Statistical
      P. R.)   Problems.'
                             JRSS Series A, Vol. 27, p. 4, 1964.

391   MOSSON, T. M.   'Some Inter-Industry Comparisons of
      (and CLARK,   the Backgrounds and Careers of
      D. G.)   Managers.'
                             B. Journ. Ind. Rel., Vol. 6, No. 2,
                             pp. 220–231, 1968.

392   MOULTON, J. S.   See No. 61.
      (with BLAKE, R.)

393   MUMFORD, ENID   *Living with a Computer.*
                             IPM, London, 1966.

394   MUMFORD, E. (and   *Computers—Planning for People.*
      WARD, T. B.)   Batsford, London, 1968.

395   MYERS, C. A. (with   See No. 226.
      HARBISON, F. H.)

396   MYERS, C. A. (with   See No. 227.
      HARBISON, F. H.)

397   NAIR, K. (with   See No. 38.
      BASA, V. S.)

398   NAM, G. B. (with   See No. 185.
      FOLGER, J. K.)

399   NAVAS, A. N.   *Managerial Manpower Forecasting and
                             Planning.*
                             Graduate School of Business, Indiana
                             Univ., 1965.

400   NEILD, R. R.   *Pricing and Employment in the Trade Cycle.*
                             NIESR, Paper 21, Cambridge Univ.
                             Press, London, 1963.

401   NELSON, P. D.   'Life Status and Interpersonal Values.'
                             Educational and Psychological Measure-

		ment, Vol. 26, No. 1, pp. 121–130, 1966.
402	NELSON, P. D.	*Attitudes of Marines during Post Enlistment*, 1966.
		Report 21, Navy Medical Neuropsychiatric Research Unit.
		Washington DC, USA, 1966.
403	NEMHAUSER, G. M. (and NUTTLE, H. L. W.)	'A Quantitive Approach to Employment Planning.'
		Management Science, Vol. II, pp. 155-165, June, 1965.
404	NEWMAN, W. H.	'Shaping the Master Strategy of your Firm.'
		California Management Review, Spring, 1967.
405	NEYMAN, J. (with FIX, E.)	See No. 181.
406	NIEHAUS, R. J. (with COOPER, W. W., and CHARNES, A.)	See No. 110.
407	NORDEN, P. V.	'Applications of the Life Cycle Model to Project Manpower Planning and Control.'
		Manpower Planning, p. 256,
		EUP, London, and American Elsevier, New York, 1966.
408	NUTTLE, H. L. W. (with NEMHAUSER, G. M.)	See No. 403.
409	O'DONOGHUE	'Manpower and Educational Activities of the Irish EIP Team.'
		Manpower Forecasting in Educational Planning.
		OECD, Paris, 1966.
410	OECD	*Productivity Measurement*, Vols. 1 and 2.
		OECD, Paris, 1955.
411	OECD	*Employment Forecasting.*
		OECD, Paris, 1963.
412	OECD	*Active Manpower Policy.*
		OECD, Paris, 1964.

413   OECD   *Manpower in Canada.*
                     OECD, Paris, 1965.

414   OECD   *Manpower Policy—Austria.*
                     OECD, Paris, 1965.

415   OECD   *Wages and Labour Mobility.*
                     OECD, Paris, 1965.

416   OECD   *Personnel Planning in Firms.*
                     OECD, Paris, 1967.

417   OECD   *The Mediterranean Regional Project—*
                     Country Reports.
                     OECD, Paris, 1967.

418   OECD   *The Overall Level and Structure of Research*
                     and Development in Member Countries.
                     OECD, Paris, 1967.

419   OECD   *Mathematical Models in Educational*
                     Planning.
                     OECD, Paris, 1967.

420   OECD   *Methods and Statistical Needs for*
        DIRECTORATE   *Educational Planning.*
        FOR SCIENTIFIC   OECD, Paris, 1967.
        AFFAIRS

421   OEEC   *Forecasting Manpower Needs for the Age of*
                     Science.
                     OEEC, Paris, 1963.

422   O'HERLIGHY,   *Labour Statistics Needed for the Estimation*
        C. ST. J.   *of Production Functions.*
                     European Conference of Statisticians,
                     1967, to be published.

423   OLSON, P. T.   *Nomograms for Army Manpower Policy*
                     Evaluations.
                     Research Publication 1147.
                     Army Personnel Research Office,
                     USA, 1966.

424   OLSON, P. T. (and   *Manpower Rotation Policy Model.*
        SORENSON, R. C.)   Research Publication 172.
                     Army Personnel Research Office,
                     USA, 1963.

425   ORCUTT, G. H.   *Microanalysis of Socio-economic Systems—*
        (GREENBERGER,   *a Simulation Study.*
        M., KORBEL, J.,   Harper and Row, New York, 1961.
        and RIVLIN, E.)

426 O'TOOLE, E. F.   'Long Range Planning and Top
                             Management Role in ADP.'
                             Financial Executive, Feb., 1966.

427 OWEN, J. P. (and   'Consequences of Voluntary Early
     BELZUNG, L. D.)   Retirement.'
                             B. Journ. Ind. Rel., Vol. 5, No. 2, pp.
                             162-189, 1967.

428 PACKARD, K. D.   *Probabilistic Forecasting of Manpower
                             Requirements.*
                             IEEE, Transactions No. 9, 1962.

429 PAGE, G. T.   *The Industrial Training Act and After*
                             André Deutsch, London, 1967.

430 PARNES, H. S.   *Forecasting Educational Needs for
                             Economic and Social Development.*
                             OECD, Paris, 1962.

431 PARNES, H. S. (ed.)   *Planning Education for Economic and
                             Social Development.*
                             OECD, Paris, 1963.

432 PARNES, H. S.   'Scope and Method of Human
                             Resource and Educational Planning.'
                             *Manpower Forecasting in Educational
                             Planning.*
                             OECD, Paris, 1966.

433 PARNES, H. S.   'Labor Force Mobility.'
                             *Lectures and Methodological Essays on
                             Educational Planning.*
                             OECD, Paris, 1966.

434 PATON, W. A.   *Accounting Theory.*
                             Accounting Studies Press,
                             Chicago, USA, 1962.

435 PAUKERT, F.   'Manpower Planning in Eastern
                             Europe.'
                             International Labour Review, August, 1962.

436 PAUKERT, F.   'The Interdependence of High-level
                             Manpower Planning and Economic
                             Planning.'
                             International Labour Review, April, 1964.

437 PAUKERT, F.   'Technical Change and the Level of
                             Employment in Western Europe.'
                             B. Journ. Ind. Rel., Vol. 6, No. 2,
                             pp. 139-155, 1968.

438 PAUL, L.   *Deployment and Pay of Clergy.*
                             Church Information Office, 1964.
439 PAYNE, B.   'Do You Plan Ahead?'
                             International Management, Vol. 18, No.
                             12, Dec., 1963.
440 PAYNE, B.   *Planning for Company Growth.*
                             McGraw-Hill, New York and
                             Maidenhead, 1963.
441 PEACOCK, A. T.   'Economic Growth and the Demand
                             for Qualified Manpower.'
                             District Bank Review, London, June, 1963.
442 PEARCE, F. T.   'Financial Effects of Labour Turnover.'
                             Studies in Economics and Society.
                             Monograph A4, University of
                             Birmingham, UK, 1967.
443 PELLING, A. A.   'Manpower Planning in the Coal
                             Industry.'
                             Personnel Management, Vol. 48, p. 376,
                             1966.
444 PERRINH, F. R.   *Long Range Planning in Business.*
                             PA Management Consultants,
                             London, 1965.
445 PHELPS BROWN,   *Economics of Labour.*
     E. H.   Yale University Press, USA, 1962.
446 PHIPPS, M.   'Laying Bare the Business Trends.'
                             Data and Control, Vol. 1, No. 8, 1963.
447 PIGORS, P. (and   *Personnel Administration.*
     MYERS, C. A.)   McGraw-Hill, New York and
                             Maidenhead, 1964.
448 PLATT, J. W.   *Education for British Management.*
                             BIM, London, 1965.
449 POIDEVIN, B. L.   'A Study of Factors Influencing
                             Labour Turnover.'
                             Personnel Practice Bulletin, Vol. 12,
                             pp. 11-18, 1956.
450 POLLARD, J. H.   'On the Use of the Direct Matrix
                             Product in Analysing Certain
                             Stochastic Population Studies.'
                             Biometrika, Vol. 53, pp. 397–415, 1966.
451 POLLARD, J. H.   'A Note on the Age Structure of
                             Learned Societies.'

		JRSS Series A, Vol. 131, Part 4, pp. 569–579, 1968.
452	PRAIS, S. J.	'Measuring Social Mobility.' *JRSS Series A*, Vol. 118, Part I, pp. 56–66, 1954.
453	PRAIS, S. J. (with HART, P.)	See No. 232.
454	PREST, A. R. (and TURVEY, R.)	'Cost Benefit Analysis—a Survey.' *Economic Journal*, Vol. 75, Dec., 1965.
455	PRESTON, L. E. (and BELL, E.)	'The Statistical Analysis of Industry Structure.' *JASA*, Vol. 56, pp. 925–932, 1961.
456	PRIESTLEY, B.	*British Qualifications.* André Deutsch, London, 1966.
457	PROULX, P. R.	'The Assessment on Long-term Manpower Requirements.' *Relations Industrielles*, Quebec, 1965.
458	PRYBYLSKI, L.	'Manpower Planning—Guides Take Out the Guesswork.' *Personnel*, AMA, New York, pp. 65-69, Jan., 1963.
459	PURKISS, C.	'Recruitment, Training, and Redeployment Planning in an Industry.' *Manpower Planning in the Defence Context.* EUP, London, and American Elsevier, New York, 1969.
460	PYKE, R.	'Markov Renewal Processes.' *Ann. Math. Stats.*, Vol. 32, pp. 1231-1259, 1961.
461	PYM, D.	'Technical Change and the Misuse of Professional Manpower.' *Occupational Psychology*, Vol. 1, No. 1, pp. 1-16, 1967.
462	PYMAN, C. L.	'Company Forward Planning.' *Works Management*, Jan., 1967.
463	QUINTON, H.	*Long-Range Planning in an Expanding Economy.* AMA, New York, USA, 1965.
464	QUIGLEY, P.	'Problems of the New Enterprise.' *Manpower and Applied Psychology*, Vol. 1, No. 1, 1967.

465 RADFORTH, J. L. (with BUZZARD, R. B.)   See No. 92.

466 RAIMON, R.   'Change in Productivity and the Skill Mix.'
International Labour Review, Vol. 92, No. 4, 1965.

467 RAIMON, R. (with STOIKOV, V.)   See No. 452.

468 REDFERN, P.   *Input-Output Analysis and its Application to Education and Manpower Planning.* HMSO, London, 1967.

469 REHMUS, F. P. (and WAGNER, H.)   'Applying Linear Programming to Your Pay Structure.'
Business Horizons, Vol. 6, No. 4, pp. 89-98, 1963.

470 RICE, A. K. (HILL, J., and TRIST, E. L.)   'Representation of Labour Turnover as a Social Process.'
Human Relations, Vol. 3, pp. 349-372, 1950.

471 RICE, A. K.   'An Examination of the Boundaries of Part Institutions.'
Human Relations, Vol. 4, pp. 393-400, 1951.

472 RICE, A. K.   'The Relative Interdependence of Sub-Institutions as Illustrated by Departmental Labour Turnover.'
Human Relations, Vol. 5, pp. 83-90, 1952.

473 RICE, A. K. (and TRIST, E.)   'Institutional and Sub-Institutional Determinants of Change in Labour Turnover.'
Human Relations, Vol. 5, pp. 347-371, 1952.

474 RIVLIN, E. (with ORCUTT, G. H., GREENBERGER, M., and KORBEL, J.)   See No. 426.

475 ROBERTS, T. J.   *Developing Effective Managers.* IPM, London, 1967.

476 ROBINSON, C. 'Some Principles of Forecasting in Business.'
J. Ind. Econ., New York, 1965.

477 ROGERS, T. G. P. *Manpower Planning.*
BIM, London, 1966.

478 ROGERS, T. G. P. 'Providing the Human Resources.'
Annual Review of Management Techniques.
Management Today, Dec., 1968.

479 ROGOFF, N. *Recent Trends in Occupational Mobility.*
The Free Press, Glencoe, Illinois, USA, 1953.

480 ROONEY, J. J. 'Developing Values in Adolescents.'
National Catholic Guidance Conference Journal, Vol. 9, No. 3, pp. 157–164, 1965.

481 ROSSOTTI, C. O. *Two Concepts of Long Range Planning.*
Boston Staff Deposit and Trust Company, Mass., USA, 1965.

482 ROUTH, G. *Occupation and Pay in Great Britain.*
Cambridge University Press, London and New York, 1965.

483 ROWE, K. H. 'An Appraisal of Appraisals.'
J. Man. Stud., Vol. 1, pp. 1–25, 1965.

484 RUITER, R. *Manpower Forecasts and Educational Planning in the Netherlands.*
OECD, Paris, 1966.

485 RUTZICK, M. (and SWERDLOFF, S.) 'The Occupational Structure of US Employment 1940–1960.'
Monthly Labor Review, Vol. 85, No. 11, p. 1209, 1962.

486 SAFEER, H. B. (ed.) *A Computed Model for a Civilian and Military Manpower.*
R–A–C paper P–13.
Research Analysis Corporation, McLean, Virginia, USA, 1965.

487 SAFEER, H. B. *Estimating Parameters for a Civilian-Manpower-Pool Projection Model.*
R–A–C Technical paper TP–219, Research Analysis Corporation, McLean, Virginia, USA, 1966.

488 SAIG, AL J. (with   See No. 322.
     LAYARD, P. R. G.)

489 ST. THOMAS, C. E.   *Practical Business Planning.*
                           AMA, New York, USA, 1965.

490 SALTER, W. E.   *Productivity and Technical Change.*
                           Cambridge University Press, London
                           and New York, 1960.

491 SANDGREN, L.   'Estimation of Manpower Require-
                           ments in the Light of Educational
                           Planning in Sweden.'
                           *Manpower Forecasting in Educational
                           Planning.*
                           OECD, Paris, 1966.

492 SCANLON, J. N.   'Profit Sharing under Collective
                           Bargaining.'
                           Industry & Labour Relations Review,
                           Vol. 2, Part 1, pp. 58-75, 1948.

493 SCHLEH, E. C.   *Management by Results.*
                           McGraw-Hill, New York and
                           Maidenhead, 1961.

494 SCHONNING, G.   'Effects of Changing Industrial
                           Structure on Occupational Trends.'
                           The Requirements of Automated Jobs.
                           Supplement, Final Report of the North
                           American Joint Conference, 1964.
                           OECD, Paris, 1965.

495 SCOTT, B. W.   *Long Range Planning in American Industry.*
                           AMA, New York, 1965.

496 SCOTT, R. W.   *Office Automation — Administrative and
                           Human Problems.*
                           OECD, Paris, 1966.

497 SCOVILLE, J. G.   *The Job Content of the Canadian Economy,
                           1941, 1951 and 1961.*
                           Special Labor Force Study No. 3.
                           Dominion Bureau of Statistics,
                           Ottawa, 1967.

498 SCOVILLE, J. G.   *The Structure of Labour Demand 1960-80.*
                           UN Inter-regional Seminar, August,
                           1966, to be published.

499 SEAL, H. L.   'The Mathematics of a Population
                           Composed of Stationary Strata each

Recruited from the Stratum below and Supported at the Lowest Level by a Uniform Annual Number of Entrants.'
Biometrika, Vol. 33, pp. 226–230, 1945.

500 SEASHORE, S. E. (with LIKERT, R.)   See No. 343.

501 SHAFFER, L. R. (RITTER, J., and MEYER, W. L.)   *The Critical Path Method.* McGraw-Hill, New York and Maidenhead, 1965.

502 SHELLY, M. (with LEAVITT, H. J. and COOPER, W. W.)   See No. 123.

503 SHEPPARD, H. L.   'An Integrated Approach to Manpower and Economic Development.' *Dimensions of Manpower Policy— Program and Research.* Johns Hopkins Press, Baltimore, US, 1966.

504 SIEGELMAN, L. (with SPENCER, M. H.)   See No. 529.

505 SILCOCK, H.   'The Phenomenon of Labour Turnover.' *JRSS Series A*, Vol. 117, pp. 429-440, 1954.

506 SILCOCK, H.   'Recording and Measurement of Labour Turnover.' *Personnel Management*, Vol. 37, pp. 71–78, June, 1955.

507 SIMON, H. A.   'Compensation of Executives.' *Sociometry*, Vol. 20, pp. 32–35, 1957.

508 SIMON, H. (with MARCH, J. G.)   See No. 364.

509 SIMONE, A. J.   'The Unnecessary Mystique Surrounding Manufacturing Progress Models.' *J. Man. Studies*, Vol. 5, Part 3, 1968.

510 SINHA, M. R.   *The Economics of Manpower Planning.* Asian Studies Press, Bombay, 1965.

511 SJOHOLM, A. A.   'Human Factors Research and Manpower Predictions.' *Manpower Planning*, pp. 68–79,

EUP, London, and American Elsevier, New York, 1966.

512　SKOROV, G.　'Manpower Approach to Educational Planning—Methods Adopted in the Centrally Planned Economies.'
Economic and Social Aspects of Educational Planning.
UNESCO, Paris, 1964.

513　SKRINDO, T.　'Manpower Planning in Norway.'
International Labor Review, Aug., 1957.

514　SMIDDY, H. F.　*Long Range Planning.*
Netherlands Inst. Voor Efficiency, The Hague, 1962.

515　SMITH, A. J.　*Redundancy Practices in Some Industries.*
OECD, Paris, 1965.

516　SMITH, A. R.　'Economic Aspects of Training.'
Manpower Planning, pp. 148-154,
EUP, London, and American Elsevier, New York, 1966.

517　SMITH, A. R.　'Manpower Planning in Management.'
Manpower & Applied Psychology, Vol. 1, No. 2, 1967.

518　SMITH, A. R.　'Manpower Planning in the Management of the Royal Navy.'
J. Man. Stud., Vol. 4, pp. 127–139, 1967.

519　SMITH, A. R.　'Defence Manpower Studies.'
ORQ, Vol. 19, pp. 257–274, 1968.

520　SMITH, A. R.　*Mathematical Models in the Management of Manpower Systems.*
EUP, London, to be published.

521　SMITH, C. S. (with ARMITAGE, P., and ALPER, P.)　See No. 6.

522　SMITH, D.　*Group Assessment Programs.*
Business Publications, London, 1966.

523　SMITH, J. H.　'Analysis of Labor Mobility.'
Manpower Policy and Employment Trends.
G. Bell and Sons, London, 1966.

524　SMITH, W. L. (with COX, D. R.)　See No. 128.

525　SOKOL, M.　'High Level Manpower Planning and

		Analysis of Czechoslovak Experience.'
		International Labour Review, Jan., 1967.
526	SOLOMON, L.	'On the Application of Compound Interest Functions to Certain Manpower Problems.'
		JIA, Vol. 74, pp. 44–48, 1948.
527	SONIN, M. (and ZHILTSOV, E.)	'Economic Development and Employment in the Soviet Union.'
		International Labour Review, Vol. 96, No. 1, p. 67, 1967.
528	SORENSON, R. C. (with OLSON, P. T.)	See No. 425.
529	SPENCER, M. H. (and SIEGELMAN, L.)	*Managerial Economics.* Irwin Press, Homewood, Ill., 1964.
530	SRIVASTAVA, R. K.	*Projecting Manpower Demands— a Review of Methodology.* Directorate of Manpower, New Delhi, India, 1964.
531	STARR, M.	'Planning Models.' *Management Science*, Dec., 1966.
532	STEIBER, J.	*Employment Problems of Automation and Advanced Technology—an International Perspective.* Macmillan, London, 1966. (US distributor, St. Martin's Press, New York.)
533	STEINDL, J.	*Random Processes and the Growth of Firms.* Griffin, London. 1965.
534	STEINDL, J.	'The Role of Manpower Requirements in the Educational Experience of the Austrian EIP team.' *Manpower Forecasting in Educational Planning.* OECD, Paris, 1966.
535	STEINER, G. A.	*Managerial Long Range Planning.* McGraw-Hill, New York and Maidenhead, 1963.
536	STEINER, G. A.	'How to assure Poor Long Range Planning for Your Company.'

		California Management Review, Summer, 1965.
537	STEINER, G. A.	*Multinational Corporate Planning.* Macmillan, New York and London, 1966.
538	STEINER, G. A.	'Long Range Planning (Concept and Implementation).' *Financial Executive*, July, 1966.
539	STEINER, G. A.	'Approaches to Long Range Planning for Small Firms.' *California Management Review*, Summer, 1967.
540	STEWART, R.	'Reactions to Appraisal Interviews.' *J. Man. Stud.*, Vol. 1, p. 25, 1965.
541	STIGLER, G. J. (with BLANK, D. M.)	See No. 62.
542	STOIKOV, V.	'Productivity and the Quality of the Labor Force, an International Comparison.' *B. Journ. Ind. Rel.*, Vol. 6, No. 2, pp. 156–165, 1968.
543	STOIKOV, V. (and RAIMON, R.)	'The Quality of the Labour Force.' *Industrial and Labor Relations Review*, April, 1967.
544	STOLLEY, H.	'An Application of Quadratic Programming in the German Air Force.' *Applications of Mathematical Programming Techniques.* EUP, London, and American Elsevier New York, 1969.
545	STONE, R. (with PYATT, C., BROWN, A., and LEICESTER, C.)	See No. 82.
546	STONE, R.	'A Model for Educational System.' *Minerva*, Vol. 3, pp. 172–186, 1965.
547	STONE, R.	'Input-Output and Demographic Accounting—a Tool for Educational Planning.' *Minerva*, Vol. 4, No. 3, Spring, 1966.

548 STONE, R. (and   'The Methodology of Planning
       LEICESTER, C.)   Models.'
                             National Economic Planning.
                             Columbia University Press, New York,
                             1967.

549 STONE, R.   'An Example of Demographic
       (and others)   Accounting—The School Age.'
                             Minerva, Vol. 6, No. 2, p. 185, 1968.

550 STONE, R.   *Demographic Accounting and Model Build-
                             ing: with Special References to Learning
                             and Earning.*
                             Mimeographed, Cambridge, 1968, to
                             be published.

551 STRAND, K. (and   'Cyclical Variations in Civilian Labor
       DERNBERG, T.)   Force Participation.'
                             Review of Economics and Statistics, Vol.
                             46, 1964.

552 STRAND, K. (with   See No. 141.
       DERNBERG, T.,
       and DUKLER, J.)

553 STRINGER, J.   *Recruitment to Ensure Management
                             Succession.*
                             Internal Document T.279.
                             Institute of Operational Research,
                             London, 1964.

554 SVERDRUP, E.   'Estimates and Test Procedures in
                             Connexion with Stochastic Models of
                             Deaths, Recoveries and Transfers be-
                             tween Different States of Health.'
                             Skand Actuar.,Vol. 46,pp. 184–211,1965.

555 SVIMEZ   *Trained Manpower Requirements for the
                             Economic Development of Italy—Targets
                             for 1975.*
                             Giuffre, Rome, 1961.

556 SWEDISH ROYAL   *Modern Swedish Labour Market Policy.*
       NATIONAL   Prisma, Stockholm, 1966.
       LABOUR MARKET
       BOARD

557 SWERDLOFF, S.   'Manpower Projection—Some Con-
                             ceptual Problems and Research Needs.'
                             Monthly Labour Review, Feb., 1966.

558   SWERDLOFF, S.   See No. 207.
      (with
      GOLDSTEIN, H.)

559   SWINTH, R. L.   'Organisational Planning.'
                          Industrial Management Review, Spring,
                          1966.

560   TAGA, Y.   'On the Limiting Distributions in
                          Markov Renewal Processes with
                          Finitely Many States.'
                          Ann. Inst. Stats. Math., Vol. 15, pp.
                          1–10, 1963.

561   TELLA, A.   'The Relation of Labor Force to
                          Employment.'
                          Industrial and Labor Relations Review,
                          Vol. 17, pp. 454-469, 1964.

562   TELLA, A.   'Age-Sex Sensitivity of Labor Force to
                          Employment.'
                          Industrial Relations, Vol. 4, pp. 69–83,
                          1966.

563   THIAS, H. H. (with See No. 167.
      EMMERIJ, L.)

564   THOMAS, B.   *Industrial Training Costs and Benefits.*
                          Research Project, London School of
                          Economics, to be published.

565   THOMAS, B.   'The International Circulation of
                          Human Capital.'
                          Minerva, Vol. 5, No. 4, pp. 479-506, 1967.

566   THOMPSON, S.   *How Companies Plan.*
                          AMA, New York, USA, 1962.

567   THORNTON, C. B.   *Long-Range Planning in our Expanding
                          Economy.*
                          AMA, New York, USA, 1963.

568   TIFFIN, J. (and   'Use of the Kuder Preference Record
      PHELAN, R. F.)   to Predict Turnover in an Industrial
                          Plant.'
                          Personnel Psychology, Vol. 6, pp. 195–
                          204, 1953.

569   TIFFIN, J. (and   *Industrial Psychology.*
      McCORMICK,   Allen & Unwin, London, 1966.
      E. J.)

570   TIMAR, J.   'High Level Manpower Planning in

		Hungary and its Relation to Educational Development.'
		International Labour Review, Oct., 1967.
571	TINBERGEN, J. and CORREA, H.)	'Quantitative Adaptation of Education to Accelerated Growth.' *Kyklos*, Vol. 15, 1962.
572	TINBERGEN, J. (and BOS, H.)	'A Planning Model for the Educational Requirements of Economic Development.' *Econometric Models of Education.* OECD, Paris, 1965.
573	TINBERGEN, J.	'Projections of Output and Employment.' *Lectures and Methodological Essays on Educational Planning.* OECD, Paris, 1966.
574	TOURAINE, A.	*Workers' Attitudes to Technical Change.* OECD, Paris, 1963.
575	TOURAINE, A.	*Workers' Attitudes to Social Changes.* OECD, Paris, 1967.
576	TRACE, L.	'How to Arrange the Future Today.' *Business*, Vol. 93, No. 1, Jan., 1963.
577	TRIST, E. L. (with RICE, A. K., and HILL, J. M.)	See No. 470.
578	TRIST, E. L. (with RICE, A. K.	See No. 473.
579	TURKISH STATE PLANNING ORGANISATION	*Manpower Requirements and Educational Programming in Turkey.* State Planning Organisation, Ankara, 1962.
580	TURVEY, R. (with PREST, R.)	See No. 454.
581	UK BOARD OF TRADE	*Board of Trade Journal.* HMSO, London, weekly.
582	UK BOARD OF TRADE	*Census of Distribution and Other Services,* 1961. HMSO, London, 1963.
583	UK CENTRAL OFFICE OF INFORMATION	*Industrial Training in the United Kingdom.* Reference Publication No. 5777. COI, London, 1967.

584   UK CENTRAL   *Monthly Digest of Statistics.*
      STATISTICAL   HMSO, London, monthly.
      OFFICE

585   UK CENTRAL   *Standard Industrial Classification.*
      STATISTICAL   Revised Edition, HMSO, London,
      OFFICE   1958.

586   UK CENTRAL   *National Income Statistics, Sources, and*
      STATISTICAL   *Methods.*
      OFFICE   HMSO, London, 1968.

587   UK CENTRAL   *National Income and Expenditure.*
      STATISTICAL   (Blue Book).
      OFFICE   HMSO, London, annually.

588   UK CENTRAL   *An Approach to Industrial Training.*
      TRAINING   Memorandum No. 5.
      COUNCIL   Ministry of Labour, London, 1965.

589   UK CENTRAL   *Report to the Minister.*
      TRAINING   HMSO, London, 1965.
      COUNCIL

590   UK CENTRAL   *An Approach to the Training and Develop-*
      TRAINING   *ment of Managers.*
      COUNCIL   HMSO, London, 1967.

591   UK CENTRAL   *Second Report to the Minister.*
      TRAINING   HMSO, London, 1967.
      COUNCIL

592   UK COMMITTEE   *Report on the Civil Service*, Vols. 1–4.
      ON THE CIVIL   (Chairman, Lord Fulton.)
      SERVICE   HMSO, London, 1968.

593   UK COMMITTEE   *Report into Higher Education.*
      ON HIGHER   (Chairman, Lord Robbins.)
      EDUCATION   HMSO, London, 1963 (Cmnd. 2154).

594   UK COMMITTEE   *Report on the 1965 Triennial Manpower*
      ON MANPOWER   *Survey of Engineers, Technologists,*
      RESOURCES FOR   *Scientists and Supporting Staff.*
      SCIENCE AND   HMSO, London, 1966 (Cmnd. 3103).
      TECHNOLOGY

595   UK COMMITTEE   *The Brain Drain.*
      ON MANPOWER   *Report of the Working Group on Migration.*
      RESOURCES FOR   HMSO, London, 1967 (Cmnd. 3417).
      SCIENCE AND
      TECHNOLOGY

596 UK COMMITTEE   *The Flow into Employment of Scientists,*
     ON MANPOWER   *Engineers, and Technologists.*
     RESOURCES FOR   HMSO, London, 1968 (Cmnd. 3760).
     SCIENCE AND
     TECHNOLOGY

597 UK COMMITTEE   *Scientific and Engineering Manpower in*
     ON SCIENTIFIC   *Great Britain, 1959.*
     MANPOWER.   HMSO, London, 1959 (Cmnd. 902).

598 UK COMMITTEE   *Long-term Demand for Scientific Man-*
     ON SCIENTIFIC   *power.*
     MANPOWER   HMSO, London, 1961 (Cmnd. 1490).

599 UK COMMITTEE   *Scientific and Technological Manpower in*
     ON SCIENTIFIC   *Great Britain, 1962.*
     MANPOWER   HMSO, London, 1963 (Cmnd. 2146).

600 UK COUNCIL FOR   *Enquiry into the Flow of Candidates in*
     SCIENTIFIC   *Science and Technology into Higher*
     POLICY   *Education.*
                         HMSO, London, 1968 (Cmnd. 3541).

601 UK DEPARTMENT   *The National Plan.*
     OF ECONOMIC   HMSO, London, 1965 (Cmnd. 2764).
     AFFAIRS

602 UK DEPARTMENT   *Statistics of Education.*
     OF EDUCATION   HMSO, London (published annually
     AND SCIENCE   or bi-annually in 6 parts.)

603 UK DEPARTMENT   *The Employment of Highly Specialised*
     OF EDUCATION   *Graduates—a Comparative Study in the*
     AND SCIENCE   *UK and the USA.*
                         HMSO, London, 1968.

604 UK DEPARTMENT   *Statistics of Education (Scotland).*
     OF EDUCATION   HMSO, London, annually.
     AND SCIENCE

605 UK DEPARTMENT   *Statistics of Science and Technology.*
     OF EDUCATION   HMSO, London, annually.
     AND SCIENCE

606 UK DEPARTMENT   *Statistics on Income, Prices, Employment,*
     OF EMPLOYMENT   *and Production.*
     AND   HMSO, London, monthly.
     PRODUCTIVITY

607 UK DEPARTMENT   *Department of Employment and Productivity*
     OF EMPLOYMENT   *Gazette.*

	AND PRODUCTIVITY	HMSO, London, monthly.
608	UK DEPARTMENT OF EMPLOYMENT AND PRODUCTIVITY	*Company Manpower Planning.* HMSO, London, 1968.
609	UK ENGINEERING INDUSTRY TRAINING BOARD	*Training of Adult Operators.* EITB, London, 1967.
610	UK ENGINEERING INDUSTRY TRAINING BOARD	*Training of Supervisors.* EITB, London, 1967.
611	UK ENGINEERING INDUSTRY TRAINING BOARD	*Report and Statement of Accounts for the period ended 31st March, 1968.* HMSO, London, 1968.
612	UK ENGINEERING INDUSTRY TRAINING BOARD	*The Training of Managers.* EITB, London, 1968.
613	UK ENGINEERING INDUSTRY TRAINING BOARD	*The Training of Professional Engineers.* EITB, London, 1968.
614	UK ENGINEERING INDUSTRY TRAINING BOARD	*Training for Engineering Craftsmen—the Module System.*
615	UK ESTIMATES COMMITTEE OF THE HOUSE OF COMMONS	*Ninth Report—Manpower Training for Industry.* HMSO, London, 1967.
616	UK GENERAL REGISTER OFFICE	*Classification of Occupations, 1966.* HMSO, London, 1966.
617	UK GENERAL REGISTER OFFICE	*Preliminary Report on the 1961 Census.* HMSO, London, 1964.
618	UK GENERAL REGISTER OFFICE	*1966 Census Reports.* HMSO, London, 1969.
619	UK MINISTRY OF LABOUR	*Training for Skill.* HMSO, London, 1958.

620   UK MINISTRY OF   *The Pattern of the Future.*
      LABOUR—   Manpower Studies No. 1.
      MANPOWER   HMSO, London, 1964.
      RESEARCH UNIT

621   UK MINISTRY OF   *The Metal Industries.*
      LABOUR—   Manpower Studies No. 2,
      MANPOWER   HMSO, London, 1965.
      RESEARCH UNIT

622   UK MINISTRY OF   *The Construction Industry.*
      LABOUR—   Manpower Studies No. 3,
      MANPOWER   HMSO, London, 1965.
      RESEARCH UNIT

623   UK MINISTRY OF   *Computers in Offices.*
      LABOUR—   Manpower Studies No. 4,
      MANPOWER   HMSO, London, 1965.
      RESEARCH UNIT

624   UK MINISTRY OF   *Electronics.*
      LABOUR—   Manpower Studies No. 5,
      MANPOWER   HMSO, London, 1967.
      RESEARCH UNIT

625   UK MINISTRY OF   *Occupational Changes in the UK*
      LABOUR—   *1951-1961.*
      MANPOWER   Manpower Studies No. 6,
      RESEARCH UNIT   HMSO, London, 1967.

626   UK MINISTRY OF   *Growth of Office Employment.*
      LABOUR—   Manpower Studies No. 7,
      MANPOWER   HMSO, London, 1968.
      RESEARCH UNIT

627   UK MINISTRY   *Glossary of Training Terms.*
      OF LABOUR   HMSO, London, 1967.

628   UK MINISTRY   *Efficient Use of Manpower.*
      OF LABOUR   HMSO, London, 1967.

629   UK MINISTRY   *Labour Turnover.*
      OF LABOUR   HMSO, London, 1967.

630   UK MINISTRY OF   *The Survey of Professional Engineers.*
      TECHNOLOGY   HMSO, London, 1967.

631   UK NATIONAL   *Job Evaluation.*
      BOARD FOR   HMSO, London, 1968.
      PRICES AND
      INCOMES

632   UK NATIONAL BOARD FOR PRICES AND INCOMES   *Payment by Results Systems.*
HMSO, London, 1968 (Cmnd. 3627).

633   UK NATIONAL ECONOMIC DEVELOPMENT COUNCIL   *Management Recruitment and Development.*
HMSO, London, 1965.

634   UK NATIONAL ECONOMIC DEVELOPMENT OFFICE   *Manpower in the Chemical Industry.*
HMSO, London, 1967.

635   UK NATIONAL ECONOMIC DEVELOPMENT OFFICE   *Your Manpower (Hotel and Catering).*
HMSO, London, 1967.

636   UK NATIONAL ECONOMIC DEVELOPMENT OFFICE   *Statistics of the Electronics Industry.*
HMSO, London, 1967.

637   UK NATIONAL ECONOMIC DEVELOPMENT OFFICE   *Labour Turnover (Food Processing).*
HMSO, London, 1968.

638   UK NATIONAL ECONOMIC DEVELOPMENT OFFICE   *Costing Your Labour Turnover (Rubber).*
HMSO, London, 1968.

639   UK NATIONAL ECONOMIC DEVELOPMENT OFFICE   *Labour Turnover (Clothing Industry).*
HMSO, London, 1968.

640   UK ROYAL COMMISSION ON MEDICAL EDUCATION   *Report of the Royal Commission.*
HMSO, London, 1968 (Cmnd. 3569).

641   UK UNIVERSITY GRANTS COMMITTEE   *First Employment of University Graduates.*
HMSO, London, annually.

642   UK UNIVERSITY GRANTS   *Returns from Universities in Receipt of Treasury Grant.*

	COMMITTEE	HMSO, London, annually.
643	UN DEPARTMENT OF SOCIAL AND ECONOMIC AFFAIRS	*Training in Public Service.* United Nations, New York, 1966.
644	US DEPARTMENT OF LABOR	*Occupational Mobility of Scientists.* Bureau of Labor Statistics, Bulletin No. 1121, Government Printing Office, Washington DC, 1953.
645	US DEPARTMENT OF LABOR	*Employment Outlook and Changing Occupational Structure in Electronics Manufacturing.* Bureau of Labor Statistics, Bulletin No. 1363, Government Printing Office, Washington DC, 1963.
646	US DEPARTMENT OF LABOR	*Employment Requirements and Changing Occupational Structure in Civil Aviation.* Bureau of Labor Statistics, Bulletin No. 1367, Government Printing Office, Washington DC, 1964.
647	US DEPARTMENT OF LABOR	*The Long Range Demand for Scientific and Technical Personnel: a Methodological Study.* Government Printing Office, Washington DC, 1965.
648	US DEPARTMENT OF LABOR	*Projections 1970—Interindustry Relationships, Potential Demand, Employment.* Bureau of Labor Statistics, Bulletin No. 1536, Government Printing Office, Washington DC, 1966.
649	US DEPARTMENT OF LABOR	*Technological Trends in Major American Industries.* Bureau of Labor Statistics, Bulletin No. 1474, Government Printing Office, Washington DC, 1966.
650	US DEPARTMENT OF LABOR	*Technology and Manpower in Design and Drafting, 1965-1975.*

Government Printing Office,
Washington DC, 1966.

651 US DEPARTMENT *Technology and Manpower in the Health*
OF LABOR *Service, 1965-1975.*
Government Printing Office,
Washington DC, 1966.

652 US DEPARTMENT *Technology and Manpower in the*
OF LABOR *Telephone Industry, 1965-1975.*
Government Printing Office,
Washington DC, 1966.

653 US DEPARTMENT *Occupational Outlook Handbook,*
OF LABOR *1966-1967.*
Bureau of Labour Statistics,
Bulletin No. 1450,
Government Printing Office,
Washington DC, 1966.

654 US DEPARTMENT *Tomorrow's Manpower Needs.*
OF LABOR Government Printing Office,
Washington DC, 1966.

655 US HOUSE OF *Improved Manpower Management in*
REPRE- *Federal Government.*
SENTATIVES Committee on the Civil Service,
Government Printing Office,
Washington DC, 1967.

656 US NATIONAL *Technology and the American Economy.*
COMMISSION ON Government Printing Office,
TECHNOLOGY, Washington DC, 1966.
AUTOMATION
AND ECONOMIC
PROGRESS

657 US NATIONAL *Measuring Job Vacancies.*
INDUSTRIAL Nat. Ind. Conf. Board,
CONFERENCE Publication SBE 97,
BOARD Washington DC, 1967.

658 US NATIONAL *The Long-Range Demand for Scientific and*
SCIENCE *Engineering Personnel.*
FOUNDATION National Science Foundation,
Washington DC, 1961.

659 US NATIONAL *Scientists, Engineers and Technicians in the*
SCIENCE *1960's: Requirements and Supply.*

	FOUNDATION	National Science Foundation, Washington DC, 1964.
660	VAIZEY, J.	'The Labor Market and the Manpower Forecaster—Some Problems.' *International Labour Review*, April, 1964.
661	VAJDA, S.	'The Stratified Semi-stationary Population.' *Biometrika*, Vol. 34, pp. 243-254, 1947.
662	VAJDA, S.	'Introduction to a Mathematical Theory of the Graded Stationary Population.' *Bulletin de l'Association des Actuaires Suisses*, Vol. 48, pp. 251-273, 1948.
663	VERNON, P. E.	'Criterion Problem in Selection and Guidance.' *Occupational Psychology*, Vol. 39, pp. 93–97, 1965.
664	VIMONT, C.	'Methods of Forecasting Employment in France, and Use of these Forecasts to work out Official Educational Programs.' *Economic Aspects of Higher Education* (ed. HARRIS, S. E.) OECD, Paris, 1964.
665	VROOM, V.	*Work and Motivation.* Wiley, New York and Chichester, 1964.
666	VROOM, V. (with MANN, F. C., and INDIK, B. P.)	See No. 359.
667	WAGNER, H. (with REHMUS, F. P.)	See No. 469.
668	WALKER, D. H.	'Labour Budgeting—an Approach to Manpower Planning.' *Personnel Management*, Vol. 48, pp. 196-198, Dec., 1966.
669	WALLIS, D.	'The Technology of Military Training.' *Manpower Planning*, pp. 81–110. EUP, London, and American Elsevier, New York, 1966.
670	WARD, T. B. (with MUMFORD, E.)	See No. 394.

671   WARREN, E. K.   'Where Long-Range Planning Goes Wrong.'
                                   Management Review, May, 1962.

672   WARREN, E. K.   *Long-Range Planning—the Executive Viewpoint.*
                                   Prentice-Hall, Englewood Cliffs, N.J., 1966.

673   WATSON, G. S. (and WELLS, W. T.)   'On the Possibility of Improving the Mean Useful Life of Items by Eliminating those with Short Lives.'
                                   Technometrics, Vol. 3, pp. 281-298.

674   WEBB, W. V.   'The Study of Defence Manpower in the Light of National Circumstances.'
                                   Manpower Research in the Defence Context. EUP, London, and American Elsevier, New York, 1968.

675   WEBSTER, A.   'Economic Models for Division of Labour.'
                                   Management Science, Vol. 12, p. 255, 1964.

676   WEDDERBURN, D.   *Enterprise Planning for Change.* OECD, Paris, 1966.

677   WEDDERBURN, D.   *Co-ordinated Technical and Manpower Planning for Change.* OECD, Paris, 1967.

678   WEIL, L.   'Functional Selection for the Stochastic Assignment Model.'
                                   Operations Research, Vol. 15, No. 6, p. 1063, 1967.

679   WEISBROD, B. A. (with CAIN, G. C., and HANSEN, W. L.)   See No. 94.

680   WELLS, W. T. (with WATSON, G. S.)   See No. 673.

681   WHISTLER, T. L. (and HARPER, S. F.)   *Performance Appraisal.* Holt, Rinehart, and Winston, New York and London, 1962.

682   WHITE, H.   'Cause and Effect in Social Mobility Tables.'
                                   Behavioral Science, Vol. 8, pp. 14-27, 1963.

683 WHITE, P. C.   'Research and Long-Range Planning for Petroleum and Petrochemicals.' *Research Management*, July, 1966.

684 WHITE, STEPHANIE   'The Process of Occupational Choice.' *B. Journ. Ind. Rel.*, Vol. 6, No. 2, pp. 166–184.

685 WHYTE, W. F.   *Money & Motivation.* Harper & Row, New York, 1955.

686 WEINER, R.   'Changing Manpower Requirements for Banking.' *Monthly Labor Review*, Vol. 85, p. 989, 1962.

687 WEIDENIUS, H.   *Supervisors at Work.* Swedish Council for Personnel Administration, Stockholm, 1958.

688 WIKSTROM, W. S.   'Planning for Manpower Planning.' *Business Management Record*, p. 30, August, 1963.

689 WILKINS, W. L.   'Attitudes and Values as Predictors of Military Performance.' *Manpower Research in the Defence Context.* EUP, London, and American Elsevier, New York, 1969.

690 WILLE, E.   *The Computer in Personnel Work.* IPM, London, 1966.

691 WILLSMER, R.   'Long-Range Corporate Planning and the Marketing Men.' *Management Decision*, Autumn, 1967.

692 WILSON, A. T. M.   'Aspects of Management Development and Training.' *BACIE Journal*, Vol. 15, No. 3, 1961.

693 WILSON, A. T. M.   'Some Sociological Aspects of Systematic Development.' *Journ. Man. Stud.*, Vol. 3, No. 1, 1966.

694 WILSON, N. A. B. (ed.)   *Manpower Research in the Defence Context.* EUP, London, and American Elsevier, New York, 1969.

695 WOLFE, H. D.   *Business Forecasting Methods.* Holt, Rinehart & Winston, New York and London, 1966.

696   WOOD, S.   'An Arithmetic Approach to Career
                                Planning.'
                                B. Journ. Ind. Rel., Vol. 3, Part 3,
                                pp. 291-300, 1965.

697   WOOL, H.   'Long-Term Projections of the Labor
                                Force.'
                                Long-Range Economic Projections.
                                Princeton, New Jersey, USA, 1954.

698   WRIGHT, R. C.   See No. 192.
       (with GALES, K.)

699   WRIGHT, R. C.   See No. 160.
       (with DURBIN, J.)

700   WYATT, D.   *Performance Appraisal and Review.*
                                Foundation for Research on Human
                                Behaviour.
                                Ann Arbor, Michigan, USA, 1958.

701   YOUNG, A. (and   'Predicting Distributions of Staff.'
       ALMOND, G.)   *Computer Journal*, Vol. 3, pp. 246–250,
                                1961.

702   YOUNG, A.   'Models for Planning Recruitment and
                                Promotion of Staff.'
                                B. Journ. Ind. Rel, Vol. 3, Part 3, pp.
                                301–310, 1965.

703   ZAHL, S.   'A Markov Process Model for
                                Follow-Up Studies.'
                                Human Biology, Vol. 27, pp. 90–120,
                                1955.

704   ZANDER, A. F.   *Performance Appraisals.*
                                Foundation for Research on Human
                                Behaviour, Ann Arbor, Michigan,
                                USA, 1963.

705   ZIDERMAN, A.   *Cost-Benefit Analysis of Industrial
                                Training.*
                                Research Project, Queen Mary
                                College, London. To be published.

706   ZYMELMAN, M. (with
       HOROWITZ, M. A.
       and
       HERRENSTADT,
       I. L.)   See No. 251.

ABBREVIATIONS

AMA	*American Management Association*
ANN. INST. STATS. MATHS.	*Annals of the Institute of Statistical Mathematics*
ANN. MATH. STATS.	*Annals of Mathematical Statistics*
BACIE	*British Association for Commercial and Industrial Education*
BIM	*British Institute of Management*
BISRA	*British Iron & Steel Research Association*
B. JOURN. IND. REL.	*British Journal of Industrial Relations*
COI	*Central Office of Information*
CRAC JOURNAL	*Careers Research and Advisory Centre Journal*
DSIR	*Department of Scientific and Industrial Research*
EUP	*English Universities Press*
HMSO	*Her Majesty's Stationery Office*
ICA	*Institute of Chartered Accountants*
ICI	*Imperial Chemical Industries*
ICWA	*Institute of Cost and Works Accountants*
IEEE	*Institute of Electronic and Electrical Engineers*
ILO	*International Labour Office*
IPM	*Institute of Personnel Management*
JASA	*Journal of the American Statistical Association*
JIA	*Journal of the Institute of Actuaries*
JIA STUD. SOC.	*Journal of the Institute of Actuaries Students Society*
J. MAN. STUD.	*Journal of Management Studies*
JRAeS	*Journal of the Royal Aeronautical Society*
JRSS	*Journal of the Royal Statistical Society*
LSE	*London School of Economics*
MIT	*Massachusetts Institute of Technology*
NAT. INST. INDUST. PSYCH.	*National Institute of Industrial Psychology*

NEDC	*National Economic Development Committee*
NEDO	*National Economic Development Office*
OECD	*Organisation for Economic Co-operation and Development*
OEEC	*Organisation for European Economic Co-operation*
ORQ	*Operational Research Quarterly*
SKAND. ACTUAR.	*Scandinavian Actuarial Journal*